Wisconsin

Bed & Breakfast Cookbook

Most Requested Recipes from Wisconsin's Unique B&Bs and Country Inns

By Becky LeJeune

For your next getaway, why not eat and sleep the local flavor?

Go ahead, discover for yourself what the locals love, whether it's a great farmers' market, kitschy art gallery or incredibly scenic hiking trail. Innkeepers of the Wisconsin Bed & Breakfast Association believe in modern-day exploration, and a comfy bed and yummy breakfast to come back to.

Choose from nearly 200 certified inns for your next adventure.

seek the unique

WisconsinBandB.com

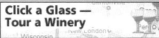
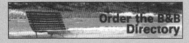
Want to stay in touch via our monthly e-newsletter? Buy a gift certificate? Order our directory? Check out specials? It's all here:

WisconsinBandB.com

seek the unique

Your Greatest Culinary Discovery could be at a Wisconsin B&B

Here in Wisconsin, we're known for being extraordinarily fun loving and uniquely friendly.

It plays out in our distinctive art of tailgating before football games, our passion for squeaky cheese curds and cheeseheads, and the micro-brews and brats that pair so nicely with them. There's a mustard museum here too, naturally. Some of our state's most original thinkers invented things that have to do with food and fun, like the ice cream sundae and the hamburger.

All of which leads us very nicely into this cookbook from the innkeepers of the Wisconsin Bed & Breakfast Association. Our Association has been certifying inns for more than 20 years, and not everyone makes the cut. Today, we're nearly 200 members strong, with every style of B&B imaginable represented in our membership — historic homes, country cabins, lake retreats, farmsteads, contemporary inns, and urban properties — each with a personality all its own. In fact, our standing invitation to visitors is "Seek the Unique."

We also thought you'd like to know that many of our innkeepers are corporate runaways who followed their inner voice that said, leave it all behind and open that inn you've always dreamed of. You won't have to ask them twice to share their insider tips for the best finds in town.

A wonderful cross-section of their most-requested recipes fills this book, reflecting their passion for locally grown goods, their penchant for fun, and their pleasure in serving up generous portions of Wisconsin hospitality. Enjoy!

Specials on the Wisconsin Menu

We're immensely proud of our farming heritage here in Wisconsin. We're America's Dairyland, home to blue skies, green fields, and an unmistakable work ethic to care for the earth just as it provides for us.

When you visit a Wisconsin B&B, you'll immediately sense the connection to the land. To find the nearest farmers' market during your stay, browse SavorWisconsin.com before you jump in the car. To find inns that have been certified by Travel Green Wisconsin for their eco-friendly practices, just click on that box when you search WisconsinBandB.com.

While you're a guest of one of our B&Bs, expect lots of culinary tips from our innkeepers. They're well versed in the language of Wisconsin food.

ARTISAN CHEESEMAKERS Wisconsin's artisan cheesemakers are leading a resurgence of handmade, small-batch specialty cheeses, reintroducing recipes that many believed were lost in the United States.

MICROBREWERIES Truth be told, long before Wisconsin became America's Dairyland, we were a beer state, thanks to the brewing know-how of German immigrants. Modern-day microbreweries still deliver "Gemütlichkeit" in a big way.

CRANBERRIES Wisconsin produces more of this tangy, tart fruit than any other state in the nation. We chose the bouncy cranberry as the featured ingredient in our recent Wisconsin Bed & Breakfast Association cook-off, with the innkeepers' winning recipes beginning on page 292.

CHERRIES Red, tart, irresistible. The Door County peninsula is famous for cherries. Late July to mid-August is harvest season for these crimson beauties.

WINERIES Yes, that's right, grape growing and wineries in Wisconsin. Family-owned vineyards produce wine in small batches from traditional or hybrid varietals.

APPLE ORCHARDS Midwest favorites like Cortland, McIntosh, Paula Red and Jonathon are grown from the Mississippi River to Lake Michigan and from Lake Superior to the state's southern-most border.

MAPLE SYRUP Hundreds of thousands of maple trees are tapped each spring to make sweet, savory Wisconsin maple syrup. Because taps are placed only an inch into the tree, there's no damage, making this a renewable treat.

While other places may have these same goodies, we happen to think they taste better here in Wisconsin.

STATE SYMBOLS

ANIMAL: Badger

BIRD: Robin

FLOWER: Wood Violet

TREE: Sugar Maple

INSECT: Honey Bee

DOG: American Water Spaniel

GRAIN: Corn

BEVERAGE: Milk

DANCE: Polka

NICKNAME: Badger State

MOTTO: Forward!

SONG: On, Wisconsin

FAMOUS WISCONSINITES

Aldo Leopold, *A Sand Country Almanac*

Senator Gaylord Nelson, founder of Earth Day

John Muir, founder of the Sierra Club

Tyne Daly

Eric Heiden

Harry Houdini

Les Paul

Liberace

Georgia O'Keefe

Tony Shalhoub—"Monk"

Spencer Tracy

Orson Welles

Gene Wilder

Laura Ingalls Wilder

Frank Lloyd Wright

GEOGRAPHICAL FEATURES OF NOTE

- Timms Hill, in Price County, is Wisconsin's highest point, at 1,952 feet above sea level.
- If laid end-to-end, Wisconsin's streams and rivers would exceed 26,000 miles, long enough to stretch around the equator.
- Wisconsin has over 14,000 lakes and 95 state parks, forests, and recreation areas.
- Horicon Marsh is a birding mecca, home to nearly 300 species of birds.
- Devil's Lake, Wisconsin's oldest state park, was established in 1911 and covers over 9,000 acres.
- The Ice Age Trail, one of eight National Scenic Trails in the country, is 1,000 miles long.

FUN FACTS ABOUT WISCONSIN

- The first-ever kindergarten in the United States was established in Watertown, Wisconsin in 1856.

- Wisconsin is the dairy capital of the U.S. and produces more milk than any other state in the nation.
- In 1884, Baraboo, Wisconsin was the location of the very first Ringling Brothers Circus.

Nobody knows mustard
like the folks at the Mustard Museum.

Since 1986, we're been tasting and enjoying mustards from all over the world. Our centerpiece collection of over 4,600 mustard jars, bottles, and tubes are on display. Our gift shop sells nearly 500 different mustards.

The bottom line — We Know Mustard!
1-800-438-6878 or
www.mustardmuseum.com

UNIQUELY WISCONSIN

Chocolate Mustard Brownies

Makes 32 servings

2 tablespoons Noyo Reserve Merlot 'n Chocolate Mustard
2 teaspoons instant espresso powder
½ pound butter or margarine
4 ounces unsweetened chocolate
2 cups brown sugar, packed
1½ cups all-purpose flour
4 eggs
2 tablespoons vanilla
1 cup chocolate chips
sifted powdered sugar

Preheat oven to 350°F. Dissolve espresso powder in the mustard and set aside. Melt butter with chocolate. Cool slightly. Add brown sugar to chocolate mixture, blend well. Then add flour and mix well. Add eggs and mix until blended. Stir in vanilla; add mustard coffee mixture. Mix until well blended. Fold in chocolate chips.

Spread in greased 13x9-inch pan. Bake 30 minutes or until tooth-pick comes out clean. Cool and cut into 32 squares. Dust with sifted powdered sugar.

Tips and Variations

You can substitute Noyo Reserve Orange Espresso Mustard.

Contents

Breads & Muffins

Breads & Muffins

You'll be tempted to make a meal
from these hearty grain breads.
The muffins burst with flavor thanks
to Wisconsin's ruby fruits such as
cranberries, cherries, and apples.

TRILLIUM

Since 1984, we have welcomed guests to our organic family farm. You know you have found a special place when you drive down the long country lane — the entrance to our farm from the nearest road. The peace and quiet are to be treasured, and no other farms can be seen from the guest cottage.

Walk the woods and fields to view abundant wildlife; explore this special part of Wisconsin with its numerous rivers, streams, and small lakes (plus Class A trout streams), state and county parks, and historic sites. Organic Valley headquarters is minutes away. Enjoy

the Kickapoo Reserve, an 8,900-acre nature preserve open to the public year-round. The Mississippi, Wisconsin, and Kickapoo Rivers are all within minutes of our farm and canoe and kayak rentals are available nearby, as are bike trails and bike rentals. Other area attractions include horseback riding, cheese factories, artisans' studios, antique shops, and fascinating restaurants to add to your pleasures.

INNKEEPER: Rosanne Boyett
ADDRESS: E10596 East Salem Ridge Road, La Farge, WI 54639
TELEPHONE: (608) 625-4492
E-MAIL: info@trilliumcottage.com
WEBSITE: www.trilliumcottage.com
ROOMS: 2 Cottages
CHILDREN: Welcome
PETS: Pet-free facility

Braided Cheese Bread

Makes 2 Large Loaves

1 tablespoon active-dry yeast	5-6 cups all-purpose flour
¼ cup warm water	1 large beaten egg
2 tablespoons honey	2 cups cream cheese
1½ cups milk	2 tablespoons sesame seeds
1½ teaspoons salt	

In a small bowl, combine the yeast, warm water, and honey. Stir together and allow to sit until the mixture is frothy and the yeast is completely dissolved. In a saucepan, heat the milk until it bubbles around the edges. Scald but do not boil. Cool the milk to a tepid temperature before adding the other ingredients. In a large mixing bowl, sift together the salt and 1 cup of flour. Stir into the cooled, scalded milk. Mix in the beaten egg and the yeast mixture. Stir in the cream cheese until the batter is uniform in texture. Add the remaining flour, one cup at a time, mixing well after each addition. Once a manageable dough has formed, turn it out onto a floured work surface. Knead, adding additional flour as needed, for 12–15 minutes, until the dough is satiny in texture. Place the dough in an oiled bowl and cover with waxed paper. Allow to raise until doubled in size (1–2 hours). Punch the dough down and divide into 6 equal portions. Working with one piece at a time, roll the dough between your hands to form a 15-inch rope. Place on a baking stone and repeat with two more portions. Pinch the ends together and braid. Cover and allow to rise in a warm spot for 35–45 minutes. Repeat the process with the remaining dough.

Preheat oven to 375°F. Brush the tops of the loaves with a bit of milk and sprinkle with sesame seeds. Bake 25–35 minutes, until golden brown on tops and bottoms. Allow the bread to cool on wire racks. Store in an airtight container at room temperature.

Augusta Victorian Rose B&B

Located exactly three blocks from the main street in Augusta, Wisconsin, the Augusta Victorian Rose B&B is a classic two-story home built in the early 1900s. The home has many traditional features including built-in bookcases, an open stairway, abundant woodwork, a fireplace, and a large sun porch. The house was renovated in 2007 and turned into a bed and breakfast with a Victorian theme and setting.

Whether sitting on the front porch listening to the clip-clip of Amish buggies going by or taking a soothing bath in one of our claw-foot tubs, our visitors should find the Augusta Victorian Rose a place of peaceful relaxation and comfort.

Within just a few miles of the Augusta Victorian Rose B&B, visitors will find several interesting area attractions including the Amish community, Dells Mill, the popular Gingerbread Jersey Cheese factory, the Woodshed, Henning Art Gallery, and Punk's Pond.

ADDRESS:	306 Baldwin Street, Augusta, WI 54722
TELEPHONE:	(715) 286-5719
E-MAIL:	victorianrose@centurytel.net
WEBSITE:	www.augustavictorianrose.com
ROOMS:	4 Rooms; Private & shared baths
CHILDREN:	Inquire
PETS:	Pet-free environment

Augusta Victorian Rose B&B Fry Bread

Makes 8 Pieces

2 cups all-purpose flour
1 teaspoon salt
2 teaspoons sugar
1 tablespoon baking powder
2 tablespoons oil
¾ cup milk or water

In a deep, heavy skillet, heat an inch or so of oil to 350°F. Mix the dry ingredients together in a big bowl. Add the oil and milk and stir to gather into a slightly sticky dough. Turn out onto a floured board and knead just 10–12 turns to bring the dough together. Pinch off a piece of dough about the size of a walnut and, with floured hands, pat the dough out between your hands to a uniform thickness. Carefully lower the piece into the hot oil. The dough will rise to the surface. Continue to cook for about a minute or so, until golden brown, and then turn and cook until golden on the second side. Remove from oil to a tray of paper towels and let drain. Repeat until all the dough is fried. Serve warm with butter and honey or use as a base for Indian tacos. Best eaten warm.

EAGLE HARBOR INN

Eagle Harbor Inn is a traditional bed and breakfast with nine rooms named for women innkeepers of Ephraim's past. The romantic Great Room features an open-beam ceiling, double whirlpool with robes, custom soaps & loofah, fireside wingchairs, and private balcony; perfect for honeymoons and anniversaries.

A wonderful homemade breakfast is served each morning and homemade afternoon treats are available each day around mid-afternoon.

The inn features an indoor pool, sauna, wifi, and workout room. Golf and honeymoon packages are available to make your stay extra special.

INNKEEPERS:	Nedd & Natalie Neddersen
ADDRESS:	9914 Water Street, Ephraim, WI 54211
TELEPHONE:	(920) 854-2121; (800) 324-5427
E-MAIL:	nedd@eagleharbor.com
WEBSITE:	www.EagleHarborInn.com
ROOMS:	9 Rooms
CHILDREN:	Inquire
PETS:	Resident pets only

Lavosh

Makes 4 Cookie Sheets

2 ½ cups flour
1 teaspoon sugar
1 teaspoon salt
²/₃ cup water
1 egg white
2 tablespoons melted butter

TOPPING
Beaten egg whites
Dried basil
Dried thyme
Sesame seeds
Poppy seeds
Granulated garlic
Salt

Preheat oven to 400°F. In a medium bowl, mix together flour, sugar, and salt. Add water, egg white, and melted butter and mix well to make a stiff dough, Knead until smooth, about 8 minutes. Divide into four equal portions and roll out until paper thin. Place each sheet of dough on a separate cookie sheet. Brush with beaten egg whites and sprinkle with toppings. Bake 8–12 minutes, until browned.

Port Washington Inn

Welcome to an historic inn that's fresh and sparkling with artistic attention to detail, food to love, complimentary beverage centers, peaceful privacy, a quiet neighborhood, views of Lake Michigan, and generous common areas to enjoy with friends. Park and walk to restaurants, nearby bike trails, the lighthouse, lakefront, and lakeside parks. The inn is also an easy drive from Cedarburg, Milwaukee, Sheboygan, Kohler, and West Bend.

Proudly certified by Travel Green Wisconsin, we operate our bed and breakfast inn in an environmentally friendly manner. Our full breakfast, gourmet picnics offered May through October, and Good Food, Good Company Saturday Night meals are all prepared from scratch using only the finest ingredients. Coffee is freshly roasted and ground, and available early morning and with breakfast.

INNKEEPERS: Rita & Dave Nelson

ADDRESS: 308 W Washington Street, Port Washington, WI 53074

TELEPHONE: (262) 284-5583

E-MAIL: stay@portwashingtoninn.com

WEBSITE: www.portwashingtoninn.com

ROOMS: 5 Rooms

CHILDREN: Facility inappropriate for children

PETS: Pet-free environment

Focaccia with Roast Red Onions

Serves 8

"Good bread makes us happy! This is our favorite focaccia topping of many we've tried. We also make pizza using this dough."

Adapted from *Books for Cooks Favorite Recipes*, books 4, 5, & 6.

3½ cups all-purpose flour

2 teaspoons salt

1⅓ cups lukewarm water

2 teaspoons yeast

1½ tablespoons olive oil

TOPPING

4 ounces Gruyère

Slivers from one onion

1 teaspoon salt

½ teaspoon coarse black pepper

3 sprigs fresh thyme

2 tablespoons olive oil

2 tablespoons extra virgin olive oil

Place 3 cups of the flour in a bowl and make a well in the center. Sprinkle the salt around the edge of the flour. Pour the water into the well and sprinkle in the yeast. Let sit 5 minutes and then stir to dissolve. Mix in enough of the flour to make a soft paste. Cover with a cloth and let sit 20 minutes, until bubbly and slightly puffed up. Add the oil and mix in the rest of the flour from the sides of the bowl. Turn the dough onto a surface floured with the remaining ½ cup of flour and knead until smooth, about 10 minutes. The dough will be sticky, but be careful not to mix in too much flour; a moist dough will bake into a lighter bread. Place back in the bowl and cover with a cloth. Let sit until double in size. Press the dough down and form into a 9-inch circle. Place the dough onto a floured baking sheet, dimpling it with your fingers, and sprinkle grated Gruyère over the top. Arrange the onion slivers decoratively over the cheese.

Cover the dough with a tea towel and let rise 20 minutes while you preheat oven to 400°F. Sprinkle with salt, coarse pepper, and thyme and then drizzle with olive oil. Bake 35–45 minutes, until golden and crusty. Transfer to a wire rack and drizzle with extra-virgin olive oil. Serve warm or at room temperature.

Port Washington Inn Cornbread

Makes 8-10 Servings

"A recipe using no wheat flour."

—INNKEEPER, *Port Washington Inn*

¼ cup plus 2 tablespoons butter, melted
1 (10 ounce) package frozen corn
1¾ cups yellow cornmeal
1 teaspoon baking powder
½ teaspoon baking soda
1 teaspoon salt
2 eggs
2 cups buttermilk

Preheat oven to 350°F. In a deep 10-inch pie plate, melt 2 tablespoons butter and add frozen corn. Let the corn thaw while mixing the batter.

In a medium bowl, combine the cornmeal, baking powder, baking soda, and salt. In a separate bowl, beat together the eggs and buttermilk. Fold the buttermilk mixture into the dry mixture. Fold in ¼ cup butter. Pour the batter into the pie plate and mix in the corn to distribute. Bake until nicely browned, cut into wedges, and serve warm.

Tips and Variations

Honey butter, maple syrup, and cranberry sauce or sorbet make great accompaniments for this bread.

Port Washington Inn Wheat Bread

Makes 2 Regular Loaves or 8 Small Loaves

"We freshly grind wheat berries for each batch of our wheat bread."

—INNKEEPER, *Port Washington Inn*

2 cups hot water

¼ cup canola oil

½ cup brown sugar

1 tablespoon salt

1 tablespoon dry yeast

1 teaspoon sugar

¾ cup warm water

3 cups whole wheat flour

3 cups unbleached flour

In a medium bowl, mix together the hot water, oil, brown sugar, salt, and wheat flour. In a separate bowl, dissolve the yeast and sugar in the ¾ cup warm water (110–120°F); allow the yeast to foam up. Once the hot mixture has cooled, stir in the yeast and enough unbleached flour to make a kneadable dough. Remove dough to a well-floured surface and knead well, until the dough is smooth and elastic. Place the kneaded dough in an oiled bowl, turning to coat, and cover with plastic wrap and a towel. Allow the dough to double in size, then punch down and make into loaves. Place in 2 9-inch loaf pans or 8 small loaf pans. Allow the dough to rise well above the loaf pans.

Preheat oven to 350°F. Bake until well browned, immediately remove and cool on wire racks. We serve this wheat bread oven toasted.

Tips and Variations

This bread freezes really well. We serve it sliced, lightly buttered, and oven toasted in a 450°F oven. Watch it carefully as it only takes a few minutes to toast.

McConnell Inn

The McConnell Inn is named for its original owner, John Mc-Connell, who built the home as his family residence in 1900. Through the years, the home was passed down to family members. The property was for sale for the first time in 1971. By 1979, five students from Ripon College owned the house and dubbed it "The Men's Club." Because of this history, we were fortunate that the

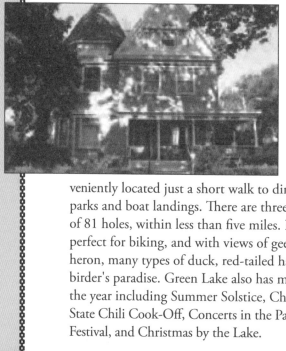

building was left in its original state; no one had done any remodeling in the 50's or 60's. We purchased the home in 1985 and opened within six months, but are always making improvements to meet the changing needs of our guests.

McConnell Inn is conveniently located just a short walk to dining, shopping, the beach, parks and boat landings. There are three golf courses, with a total of 81 holes, within less than five miles. Backcountry roads are perfect for biking, and with views of geese, sandhill cranes, blue heron, many types of duck, red-tailed hawks, and eagles, we are a birder's paradise. Green Lake also has many celebrations throughout the year including Summer Solstice, Chalk Art Festival, Wisconsin State Chili Cook-Off, Concerts in the Park summer series, Harvest Festival, and Christmas by the Lake.

INNKEEPERS:	Scott & Mary-Jo Johnson
ADDRESS:	497 S Lawson Drive, Green Lake, WI 54941
TELEPHONE:	(920) 294-6430; (888) 238-8625
E-MAIL:	info@mcconnellinn.com
WEBSITE:	www.mcconnellinn.com
ROOMS:	5 Rooms
CHILDREN:	Facility inappropriate for children
PETS:	Resident pets only

Buttermilk Chocolate Bread with Chocolate Honey Butter

Makes 1 Loaf

"This is a tasty bread, but I always make extra loaves because it makes even better French toast. It can also be made into muffins."
—INNKEEPER, *McConnell Inn*

1 cup sugar
½ cup margarine, softened
2 eggs
1 cup buttermilk
1¾ cups flour
½ cup cocoa
½ teaspoon baking powder
½ teaspoon salt
½ teaspoon baking soda
⅓ cup chopped walnuts
    dredged in 1 tablespoon flour
½ cup butter, softened
2 tablespoons chocolate flavored syrup
2 tablespoons honey

Preheat oven to 350°F. In a medium bowl, combine the sugar and margarine and blend well. Mix in the eggs and then the buttermilk. Add the flour, cocoa, baking powder, salt, and baking soda and mix until well blended. Fold in the nuts and pour the batter into a greased 8x4-inch bread loaf and bake 55–60 minutes, or until a tester comes out clean.

For the Chocolate Honey Butter: Using an electric mixer, combine the butter, chocolate syrup, and honey at high speed until the mixture is light and fluffy. Serve with sliced bread.

HAVENLY INN

Your turn-of-the-century experience awaits! Imagine a spacious great room, tiger oak dining room, three bedrooms, two bathrooms, separate hot tub room, and a complete office all to yourself. Bring guests or stay alone, either way the place is completely yours. You are precious; the Havenly Inn is timeless.

All room rates include a full gourmet-style breakfast as well as wine and appetizers each evening.

INNKEEPER:	Shaun Schmiling
ADDRESS:	519 3rd Street, Algoma, WI 54201
TELEPHONE:	(920) 487-0217
E-MAIL:	innkeeper@havenlyinn.com
WEBSITE:	www.havenlyinn.com
ROOMS:	3 Rooms; Private & shared baths
CHILDREN:	Inquire
PETS:	Pet-free environment

Lemon Berry Bread

Makes 1 Loaf

*"We do have guests every so often who are diabetic
and concerned about their sugar intake. This recipe is loved
by both diabetics and non-diabetics alike."*

—INNKEEPER, *The Havenly Inn*

⅓ cup canola oil

⅔ cup plus ½ cup sugar, divided

2 tablespoons lemon extract

1 egg

2 egg whites

1½ cups flour

1 teaspoon baking powder

½ cup skim milk

1 cup fresh blueberries

2 tablespoons grated lemon rind

½ cup lemon juice

Preheat oven to 350°F and coat a 9x5x3-inch loaf pan with
non-stick cooking spray. In a large bowl, mix the oil, ⅔ cup
sugar, lemon extract, egg, and egg whites. In a separate small bowl,
mix the flour with the baking powder. Add the flour mixture to
the sugar mixture alternately with the milk, stirring just until
blended. Fold in the blueberries and lemon rind. Pour the batter
into the prepared pan and bake 40–50 minutes, or until a toothpick inserted in the center comes away clean. Immediately upon
removing the loaf from the oven, poke holes at 1-inch intervals
on the top of the bread. In a saucepan over medium heat, mix the
remaining ½ cup sugar and lemon juice, heating until the sugar is
dissolved. Pour the warm lemon juice mixture over the bread, let
cool, and slice to serve.

FRANKLIN STREET INN

*"Every bite of Judy's breakfast brought an explosion
to our taste buds, what a treat!"* —GUEST

*"Judy has collected many recipes to offer guests
with special dietary needs."* —GUEST

The award-winning 1897 Victorian Franklin Street Inn, located
in the downtown historical district of Appleton, begins its 15th
year. We aim to go beyond your expectations to guarantee a pleasur-
able stay and we want to thank our guests for voting the inn Best
B & B in the Fox Valley for 2008.

Each of our four rooms/suites has been decorated with great
attention to detail. Whatever amenities you value most in your bed
and breakfast experiences, just look for it here because we have it:
on-site massage, whirlpools, fireplaces, and your reservation includes
a full, scrumptious breakfast served in our formal dining room or
in your suite. Enjoy the antique décor throughout the house; it
combines the elegance of the 19th century with the amenities of
the 21st. Open our door for charm and hospitality!

INNKEEPERS:	Judy & Ron Halma
ADDRESS:	318 East Franklin Street, Appleton, WI 54911
TELEPHONE:	(920) 993-1711; (888) 993-1711
E-MAIL:	info@franklinstreetinn.com
WEBSITE:	www.franklinstreetinn.com
ROOMS:	4 Rooms
CHILDREN:	Children age 5 and older welcome
PETS:	Pet-free environment

Zucchini, Pineapple, Date, Nut Bread

Makes 2 Loaves

"Our herb likes to feature Wisconsin grown produce, fresh from the garden, or shredded for a frozen winter treat. I don't want my bread to be dry or fall apart; adding the crushed pineapple not only enhances the flavor, but also keeps it moist."

—*INNKEEPER, Franklin Street Inn*

3 eggs
1 cup canola oil
2 cups sugar
2 teaspoons vanilla extract
2 cups zucchini, unpeeled and shredded
1 cup pineapple, crushed and drained
2 teaspoons baking soda
1½ teaspoons cinnamon
1 teaspoon salt
¾ teaspoon nutmeg
¼ teaspoon baking powder
1 cup chopped dates
1 cup chopped walnuts
3 cups flour

Preheat oven to 350°F. Grease, flour, and line two loaf pans with enough wax paper to cover the pan bottom (will prevent bread from sticking). Beat together the eggs, oil, sugar, and vanilla until well blended. Stir in the remaining ingredients and mix well by hand. Pour into the pans and bake 1 hour, or until a toothpick inserted in the center comes away clean. Cool on a rack for 10 minutes before removing from pans.

Eagle Centre House B&B

L et's pretend the year is 1846 and you're a weary traveler approaching an inn. Today's traveler seeks respite too! So, relax and enjoy the best life had to offer over 160 years ago, enhanced with today's finest amenities. Eagle Centre is a replica

of an 1846 Greek Revival stagecoach inn furnished in authentic period antiques and situated on 20 scenic acres. Wood-burning stoves, fireplaces, and double whirlpools add comfort. A full breakfast is included with any stay and is served on antique Tea-Leaf china.

Eagle Centre is located in the Southern Kettle Moraine Forest, a location that offers hiking, biking, skiing, and horse trails. Chicago is just two hours away, Milwaukee just under an hour. Other nearby attractions include Lake Geneva, Madison, Ten Chimneys, and Old World Wisconsin.

INNKEEPERS:	Riene Wells Herriges & Dean Herriges
ADDRESS:	W370 S9590 State Road 67, Eagle, WI 53119
TELEPHONE:	(262) 363-4700
E-MAIL:	info@eagle-house.com
WEBSITE:	www.eagle-house.com
ROOMS:	5 Rooms
CHILDREN:	Children age 12 and older welcome
PETS:	Pet-free environment

Pumpkin Bread

Makes 1 Loaf

½ cup salad oil
½ cup water
1½ cups sugar
2 eggs
1 cup pumpkin
$1^2/_3$ cups flour
½ teaspoon cloves
½ teaspoon cinnamon
½ teaspoon nutmeg
1 teaspoon baking soda
1 teaspoon baking powder
1 cup raisins, (optional)
½ cup nuts, (optional)

Preheat oven to 350°F. Grease and flour a 9x5-inch loaf pan. In a small bowl, whisk together the oil and water. In a large bowl, combine the sugar, eggs, and pumpkin. Sift together the flour, cloves, cinnamon, nutmeg, baking soda, and baking powder. Add the flour mixture to the pumpkin mixture and mix to combine. Add the oil/water mixture and stir to incorporate. Fold in the raisins and nuts and pour into the prepared pan. Bake 1 hour, or until a knife inserted in the center comes away clean.

WESTPHAL MANSION INN

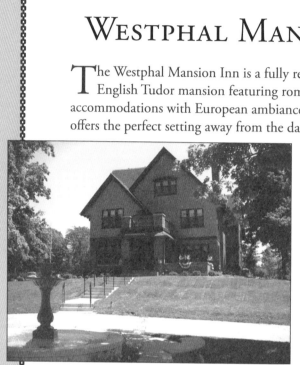

The Westphal Mansion Inn is a fully restored and stately 1913 English Tudor mansion featuring romantic and luxurious accommodations with European ambiance. The charm of the inn offers the perfect setting away from the daily distractions of life and is a comfortable haven for a romantic getaway, travelers on business, or an elegant retreat. Each of the inn's eight unique suites is tastefully furnished in an old-world French-country style. Fine linens, antiques, fireplaces, air bubble massage tubs, and other upscale amenities can be found throughout.

In the morning, enjoy a delicious four-course breakfast with dessert. English afternoon teas and wine and cheese social hours are also offered. Stroll through the English gardens and make a wish at the 1917 fountain, or cozy up with a good book or a game of chess next to a crackling fire in the grand living room.

The inn is conveniently located within walking distance of Hartford's downtown shopping, theaters, and unique restaurants.

INNKEEPERS:	Garret & Pam Terpstra
ADDRESS:	90 S Main Street, Hartford, WI 53027
TELEPHONE:	(262) 673-7938
E-MAIL:	terpstra7938@sbcglobal.net
WEBSITE:	www.westphalmansioninn.com
ROOMS:	8 Rooms
CHILDREN:	Inquire
PETS:	Resident pets only

Thelma's Banana Nut Bread

Makes 1 Loaf

*"Thelma's Banana Bread recipe has been passed down
for 3 generations. Over the past years, as a nanny
for a family of seven, I have enjoyed many afternoons
making this keepsake recipe with the third generation of children."*

—INNKEEPER, *Westphal Mansion Inn*

½ cup vegetable oil
1 cup sugar
2 eggs, beaten
3 ripe bananas mashed to a pulp
3 tablespoons milk
½ teaspoon vanilla extract
2 cups flour
1 teaspoon baking soda
½ teaspoon baking powder
½ teaspoon salt
½ cup mini chocolate chips, (optional)
½ cup chopped nuts, (optional)

Preheat oven to 350°F. In a medium bowl, beat together the oil
and sugar. Add the eggs, bananas, milk, and vanilla and mix to
combine. In a separate bowl, sift together the flour, baking soda,
baking powder, and salt. Mix the dry ingredients into the wet
mixture and fold in the chocolate chips and nuts. Grease a 9x5-
inch loaf pan and place a waxed paper sheet on the bottom of the
pan. Pour in the batter and bake 1 hour. Allow the bread to cool
5 minutes on a wire rack before removing from pan.

Tips and Variations

This recipe can be adapted for muffins. Simply bake 20 minutes at
350°F. Makes 2 dozen.

WHITE LACE INN

The White Lace Inn bed and breakfast is nestled in a quaint neighborhood in the heart of historic Sturgeon Bay, Wisconsin, on the well-known Door Peninsula. Innkeepers Dennis and Bonnie Statz and their staff invite guests to relax in one of their eighteen lovingly decorated Victorian rooms and suites. King

and queen-size Victorian beds offer sweet dreams, and soothing colors with coordinated wallpapers create an inviting atmosphere. Each room has a private bath. Twelve of the rooms include oversize whirlpools and fifteen have a fireplace, while nine of the accommodations have both. A number of the rooms also feature porches or patios.

Each morning guests are treated to a delicious breakfast to start their day. Stroll through the beautifully landscaped, park-like setting and follow the redbrick path to a gazebo at the heart of the complex, the setting for more than 1,200 weddings since 1982.

We look forward to your visit.

INNKEEPERS:	Dennis & Bonnie Statz
ADDRESS:	16 N 5th Avenue, Sturgeon Bay, Door County, WI 54235
TELEPHONE:	(920) 743-1105; (877) 948-5223
E-MAIL:	Romance@WhiteLaceInn.com
WEBSITE:	www.WhiteLaceInn.com
ROOMS:	18 Rooms
CHILDREN:	Inquire
PETS:	Pet-free environment

Mary's Holiday Cherry Almond Bread

Makes 3 Small or 2 Large Loaves

1 (8 ounce) package cream cheese
1 cup butter
1½ cups sugar
1½ teaspoons almond extract
4 eggs
2½ cups flour
1½ teaspoons baking powder
1 cup chopped almonds
3 cups rinsed and drained Door County cherries

Preheat oven to 350°F and grease 3 small or 2 large bread pans. In a medium bowl, cream together the cream cheese, butter, sugar, and almond extract. Add the eggs, one at a time, beating well after each addition. In a separate bowl, sift together the flour and baking powder. Add the flour mixture to the creamed mixture and combine. Fold in the nuts and the cherries and divide the batter evenly between the prepared pans. Bake 50-60 minutes, or until a toothpick inserted in the center comes away clean.

Tips and Variations

Tossing the nuts in a bit of flour before adding them to the batter will help to suspend them in the loaves and keep them from sinking to the bottom.

Pistachio
Chocolate Chunk Muffins

Makes 1 Dozen

1 cup flour
1 box Duncan Hines
   Butter Golden Cake Mix
1 (3.4 ounce) package
   pistachio instant pudding
4 eggs, beaten
1 cup sour cream
¼ cup water
¼ cup oil
1 large Hershey candy bar,
   chopped into chunks

Preheat oven to 400°F and grease or line regular muffin cups. In a medium bowl, sift together the flour and the cake mix. Add the instant pudding and stir together. Add the eggs to the mixture and stir. Mix in the sour cream, water, and oil, combining well. Fold in the chocolate chunks. Spoon the batter into the prepared muffin cups, filling about ⅔ full. Sprinkle additional sugar over the top and bake 15 minutes.

Strawberry Rhubarb Muffins

Makes 1 Dozen

3 cups flour
¾ cup white sugar
3¼ teaspoons baking powder
3 eggs
¾ cup milk
¼ cup oil
¼ cup sour cream
2 cups chopped rhubarb
1 cup chopped strawberries
Chopped nuts, (optional)

Preheat oven to 425°F and line muffin cups. In a medium bowl, sift together the flour, sugar, and baking powder. In a separate bowl, beat together the eggs, milk, oil, and sour cream. Add the creamed mixture to the dry ingredients and blend well. Fold in the rhubarb and strawberries. Spoon the batter into the muffin cups, filling about ¾ of the way. Sprinkle additional sugar and chopped nuts over the tops of the muffins and bake 20 minutes.

Tips and Variations

If you are using frozen strawberries, be sure to thaw and drain them before adding them to the batter.

Justin Trails
B&B Resort

This certified green inn is set in a private valley of the Drift-less Region of southwest Wisconsin, surrounded by miles of groomed hiking, mountain bike, cross-country ski, and snowshoe trails as well as two disc-golf courses; absolute heaven to anyone seeking recreation, relaxation, and rejuvenation.

The inn, which can comfortably accommodate up to eighteen guests, features three guest suites and three log cabins with whirl-pools and fireplaces. Breakfast is served each morning in the Lodge, or your room. Justin Trails prides itself in its clean, green environment and is perfect for weddings, anniversary, and birthday parties.

INNKEEPERS: Don & Donna Justin

ADDRESS: 7452 Kathryn Avenue, Sparta, WI 54656

TELEPHONE: (608) 269-4522; (800) 488-4521

E-MAIL: info@justintrails.com

WEBSITE: www.justintrails.com

ROOMS: 3 Suites; 3 Cabins

CHILDREN: Welcome

PETS: Welcome

Gluten & Dairy Free Cranberry Orange Muffins
Makes 18 Muffins

*"This recipe is an original created by my own need to eat gluten
and dairy free. The orange juice, extract, and Craisins give
a great flavor and texture to the muffins. All guests like these and
the gluten-free person feels happy to fit into the menu."*
—INNKEEPER, Justin Trails

2 cups gluten-free flour
1 teaspoon aluminum-free baking powder
1 teaspoon baking soda
½ teaspoon sea salt
1 cup orange juice
½ cup honey
⅓ cup vegetable oil
2 eggs
2 drops orange baking emulsion,
    or ½ teaspoon orange extract
½ cup Craisins
½ cup granulated organic sugar

Preheat oven to 350°F. In a medium bowl, combine the flour,
baking powder, baking soda, and salt. In a separate bowl, mix
together the orange juice, honey, oil, eggs, and orange emulsion.
Add the liquid mixture to the dry mixture and blend just until
combined. Fold in the Craisins. Use an ice cream scoop to fill
lined or greased muffin cups about ⅔ full. Top with granulated
organic sugar and bake 12–15 minutes.

Fargo Mansion Inn

The Fargo Mansion Inn is an elegant Queen Anne Victorian mansion listed on the National Historic Registry. The inn is the perfect romantic getaway. Each of the inn's private baths features hand-laid Italian marble and double whirlpool baths. A full breakfast is served each morning and you can sit and enjoy a complimentary beverage while you relax on the inn's great wrap-around porch.

Fargo Mansion is conveniently located just two blocks from the Lake Mills Town Square and a short drive from Madison, Milwaukee, and Chicago. Also nearby are the Aztalan State Park, Rock Lake, and Glacial Drumlin bike trail. So as Barry and Tom say, come and relax and make yourself at home!

INNKEEPERS:	Barry Luce & Tom Boycks
ADDRESS:	406 Mulberry Street, Lake Mills, WI 53551
TELEPHONE:	(920) 648-3654
E-MAIL:	fargo@charter.net
WEBSITE:	www.fargomansion.com
ROOMS:	5 Rooms
CHILDREN:	Facility inappropriate for children
PETS:	Resident pets only

Barry's Very Berry Muffins

Makes 1 Dozen

"We have used this recipe for over 20 years.
We wanted something simple to make breakfast preparation easier.
We came up with this basic white muffin recipe that could be
easily adapted for seasonal fruits. Repeat guests often want to know
if we are making our "Very Berry" muffins—
they are not afraid to ask for the leftovers."

—INNKEEPER, The Fargo Mansion Inn

1½ cups flour
½ cup sugar
2 teaspoons baking powder
½ teaspoon salt
1 egg
½ cup milk
½ stick butter, melted
1½ cups berries of choice, or combination

Preheat oven to 375°F and grease the cups of a muffin tin. In a large mixing bowl, sift together the dry ingredients. Add the milk, egg, and butter; mix. Fold in berries of choice. Scoop the batter into the muffin cups, filling each about ½ full. Sprinkle a bit of sugar over the top of each muffin before baking for a crispy top. Bake 20–25 minutes, or until done.

Tips and Variations

For fall, add ½ can pumpkin pie filling, 1 teaspoon cinnamon, and 1 teaspoon nutmeg in place of the berries for Pumpkin Muffins.

FEATHERED STAR B&B

The Feathered Star is located in the township of Egg Harbor, in the center of beautiful Door County, and near some of the area's prime attractions. Feathered Star is a great place for a quiet

and comfortable vacation. The inn also welcomes both pets and children.

Each of the inn's six bedrooms features a different theme and is completely handicapped accessible. Four of the rooms have semi-private sitting decks, and all have private exterior entrances. All of the bathrooms are handicapped accessible with either a shower or shower/tub with fold-down seat and hand-held nozzle. The b&b also has a whirlpool room and a common gathering room.

INNKEEPER:	Sandy Chlubna
ADDRESS:	6202 State HWY 42, Egg Harbor, WI 54209
TELEPHONE:	(920) 743-4066; (877) 743-4066
E-MAIL:	sandrac@itol.com
WEBSITE:	www.featheredstar.com
ROOMS:	6 Rooms
CHILDREN:	Welcome
PETS:	Welcome

Hawaiian Banana Nut Muffins

Makes 8-10 Jumbo Muffins

2½ cups flour
¾ cup sugar
1¼ teaspoons baking powder
1¼ teaspoons baking soda
1 teaspoon salt
3 eggs, beaten
²/₃ cup butter, melted
²/₃ cup buttermilk or yogurt
1¼ cups mashed bananas (3 medium)
²/₃ cup chopped macadamia nuts or walnuts

Preheat oven to 350°F. In a large bowl, sift together the flour, sugar, baking powder, baking soda, and salt. In a smaller bowl, blend together the eggs, butter, and buttermilk. Add the bananas to the egg mixture. Make a well in the center of the flour mixture and pour in the banana mixture; mix lightly. Fold in the nuts and spoon the batter into jumbo muffin cups, filling them ½ full. Bake 20–25 minutes.

THE CREAM PITCHER B&B

Guests of The Cream Pitcher experience a true retreat in nature. Situated among the hills of Richland County, this unglaciated area offers awesome beauty as well as outdoor activities for every season. There are more than three miles of hiking trails through the 100 acres of woodland. Watch deer, turkeys, and other wildlife and see the many species of birds while you enjoy the creek that flows close by.

The Cream Pitcher has been meticulously handcrafted to ensure the proper blend between modern amenities and old-fashioned quality and comfort. Each of the inn's four rooms has a unique and singular décor. Jared's Room is a spacious, masculine room with its own private entrance and screened porch with hammock chairs, while Katie's Room is an inviting, feminine room with a window seat where you can enjoy the panoramic view or relax and read a book. Rooms on the lower level are named after Vern's great-great-grandparents who settled here in 1854: Andrew's Room has a distinct French-country look and Tolena's Room is a happy room with a handmade log headboard that graces the king-size bed.

INNKEEPERS:	Vern & Diane Dalberg
ADDRESS:	16334 Gault Hollow Road, Blue River, WI 53518
TELEPHONE:	(608) 536-3607; (866) 391-2900
E-MAIL:	crmptchr@mwt.net
WEBSITE:	www.mwt.net/~crmptchr
ROOMS:	4 Rooms
CHILDREN:	Inquire
PETS:	Pet-free environment

Burst O' Lemon Muffins

Makes 1 Dozen

1¾ cups flour
¾ cup sugar
1 teaspoon baking powder
1 teaspoon baking soda
1 cup lemon yogurt
1 egg
⅓ cup butter or margarine, melted
1 tablespoon grated lemon peel
1 tablespoon lemon juice
½ cup flaked coconut

TOPPING
⅓ cup lemon juice
¼ cup sugar
¼ cup flaked coconut, toasted

Preheat oven to 400°F. In a large bowl, combine the flour, sugar, baking powder, and baking soda. In a separate bowl, beat together the yogurt, egg, butter, lemon peel, and lemon juice until smooth. Stir the mixture into the dry ingredients just until moistened. Fold in the coconut and fill greased or lined muffin cups ⅔ full. Bake 18–22 minutes, or until golden brown and muffins test done. Cool 5 minutes before removing to wire racks.

For the topping: In a saucepan, combine the lemon juice and sugar. Cook, stirring until the sugar dissolves. Stir in the toasted coconut. Using a toothpick, poke 6–8 holes in each muffin. Spoon the lemon coconut mixture over the muffins. Serve warm or cool to room temperature.

Black Walnut Guest House

Discover one of Door County's hidden treasures. The Black Walnut Guest House in Sturgeon Bay is a welcoming four-room bed and breakfast. Each room has been uniquely designed and tastefully decorated and includes a double whirlpool tub, fireplace, small refrigerator, and private bath. A warm continental breakfast consisting of homemade muffins, fresh fruit, hot and cold cereal, yogurt, homemade granola, juice, coffee, and tea is served to your door each morning.

The Black Walnut Guest House is situated in a quiet neighborhood one half-block from one-of-a- kind Jefferson Street shops, and just a short walk from Sturgeon Bay's Historic Downtown. Discover the Door County Historical, Maritime, and Fairfield museums, The Miller Art Museum, Third Avenue Playhouse, and both fine and casual dining.

INNKEEPERS:	Geri Ballard & Mike Shatusky
ADDRESS:	454 N 7th Avenue, Sturgeon Bay, WI 54235
TELEPHONE:	(920) 743-8892; (877) 255-9568
E-MAIL:	stay@blackwalnut-gh.com
WEBSITE:	www.blackwalnut-gh.com
ROOMS:	4 Rooms
CHILDREN:	Inquire
PETS:	Resident pets only

Morning Glory Muffins

Makes 12 Muffins

*"This recipe was passed down from my mom, along with
all of her other muffin recipes, when we bought my parents' b&b,
The Barrington Inn on Block Island, in Rhode Island."*
—INNKEEPER, Black Walnut Guest House

3 eggs
1 cup vegetable oil
½ teaspoon vanilla extract
1¼ cups sugar
2 cups flour
2 teaspoons baking soda
½ teaspoon salt
2 teaspoons cinnamon
1½ cups shredded carrots
2 large apples, chopped
¾ cup shredded coconut
½ cup raisins, (optional)
½ cup pecans

Preheat oven to 375°F. In a large bowl, cream together the eggs,
oil, and vanilla. Beat until well blended. Add the sugar and mix to
combine. In a separate bowl, sift together the flour, baking soda,
salt, and cinnamon. Add the flour mixture to the batter and beat
well. Fold in the carrots, apples, coconut, raisins, and pecans.
Divide the batter evenly among greased or lined muffin cups and
bake 18–25 minutes.

APPLE TREE LANE B&B

Imagine escaping to a beautiful place rich in history, tradition and comfortable elegance.

Let the Apple Tree Lane Bed & Breakfast welcome you to their 1880's Victorian farmhouse located on seven acres along the Crystal River. Inside this beautiful home you will enjoy the comforts of five large guest suites, each with private attached baths and luxury amenities.

A gourmet candlelit breakfast, often featuring the inn's signature apple creations, often served mornings in the formal dining room, set with crystal, china, and silver. Guests may also breakfast in their room or on the covered porch if they choose.

INNKEEPERS: **Michael & Kerri Thiel**

ADDRESS: **E3192 Apple Tree Lane, Waupaca, Wisconsin 54981**

TELEPHONE: **(715) 258-3107; (877) 277-5316**

E-MAIL: **thielkerri@aol.com**

WEBSITE: **www.appletreelanebb.com**

ROOMS: **5 Rooms**

CHILDREN: **Children age 10 and older welcome**

PETS: **Pet-free environment**

Apple Streusel Muffins

Makes 16 Muffins

1½ cups quick oats
1 cup all-purpose flour
½ cup sugar
¾ teaspoon salt
2½ teaspoons baking powder
½ teaspoon baking soda
1 teaspoon cinnamon
1 egg, lightly beaten
1 cup milk
3 tablespoons butter
1½ cups cored, peeled, and
  diced apples of choice

STREUSEL
½ cup oats, regular not quick
2 tablespoons firmly packed
  brown sugar
2 tablespoons butter

CARAMEL DRIZZLE
½ cup dark brown sugar
3 tablespoons butter
2 tablespoons cream
½ cup powdered sugar

Preheat oven to 400°F. Process the oats in a food processor for
2 minutes. In a bowl, combine the processed oats, flour, sugar,
salt, baking powder, baking soda, and cinnamon. Make a well
in the center and add the egg, milk, and butter. Stir just until
moistened and fold in the apples. Fill greased muffin cups ⅔ full.
In a small bowl, blend together all of the streusel ingredients using
a fork. Sprinkle over the tops of the muffins and bake 15–20 minutes.

For the caramel drizzle: While the muffins bake, place all of the
caramel drizzle ingredients, except the powdered sugar, together
in a saucepan and bring to a boil over medium-high heat. Cook
and stir 2 minutes. Remove from heat and blend in the powdered
sugar. Remove the muffins and cool slightly before drizzling with
caramel. Enjoy!

BLACKSMITH INN
ON THE SHORE

Nestled on the Lake Michigan shore in the charming village of Baileys Harbor, Wisconsin, the Blacksmith Inn On the Shore graciously blends Door County bed and breakfast charm with contemporary amenities. Unwind and relax in one of fifteen deliciously private guest rooms, each with an in-room whirlpool, fireplace, private balcony, and extraordinary harbor view.

Our local knowledge of the Door Peninsula is sure to enhance your romantic escape. Choose the serenity of strolling, biking, hiking, or kayaking to fulfill your getaway cravings. Or immerse yourself in all the Peninsula has to offer including miles of shoreline, lighthouses, music festivals, theater venues, art galleries, unique gift shops, wineries, and a wealth of dining experiences.

INNKEEPERS:	Joan Holliday & Bryan Nelson
ADDRESS:	8152 HWY 57, Baileys Harbor, WI 54202
TELEPHONE:	(800) 769-8619
E-MAIL:	relax@theblacksmithinn.com
WEBSITE:	www.theblacksmithinn.com
ROOMS:	15 Rooms; 1 Cottage
CHILDREN:	Facility inappropriate for children
PETS:	Resident pets only

Blacksmith Inn
Pumpkin Pecan Muffins

Makes 10 Medium Muffins

*"This recipe is Bryan's mother's pumpkin bar recipe
to which she adds a thick layer of cream cheese frosting."*
—INNKEEPER, *Blacksmith Inn On the Shore*

1 cup sugar
½ teaspoon baking soda
1 teaspoon baking powder
½ teaspoon salt
1 teaspoon cinnamon
¼ teaspoon cloves
1 cup flour
1 egg
½ cup oil
1 cup canned pumpkin
¼ cup chopped pecans
¼ cup raisins

Preheat oven to 325°F and grease or line 10 standard muffin cups. In a medium mixing bowl, thoroughly combine the sugar, baking soda, baking powder, salt, cinnamon, cloves, and flour. Mix in the egg, oil, and pumpkin. Fold in the pecans and raisins. Fill the prepared muffin cups ⅔ full and sprinkle the tops with cinnamon sugar. Bake 20–25 minutes.

Inn at Pinewood

The Inn at Pinewood is a former classic 1934 log hunting and fishing lodge. The original sienna log walls remain and the hulking fieldstone fireplace has no doubt heard its share of fish tales. Sit by the fire to chat, read, or just relax. The large common area is filled with antiques and is a great place to hold a meeting, family reunion, or small wedding, yet is still cozy enough for two.

Enjoy breakfast in the sunlit garden room and you may get the chance to see Northwoods wildlife. After breakfast take advantage of the watercraft available for rent, join the loons on private Carpenter Lake, and watch the eagles perch in the trees. At night, sit around the fire pit to count stars and enjoy the peace and quiet that our guests say is abundant.

INNKEEPERS: Jane & Bill Weber

ADDRESS: 1820 Silver Forest Lane, Eagle River, WI 54521

TELEPHONE: (715) 477-2377

E-MAIL: pinewood@nnex.net

WEBSITE: www.inn-at-pinewood.com

ROOMS: 8 Rooms

CHILDREN: Inquire

PETS: Resident pets only

Coffee Cake Muffins

Makes 1 Dozen

"This muffin was featured in an article about the Inn at Pinewood in Midwest Living Magazine *in 2002 and again in 2007 when it was picked as one of* Midwest Living's *'20 Best Recipes of All Time.' It's our most requested muffin."*

—INNKEEPER, *Inn at Pinewood*

1½ cups flour
½ cup sugar
2 teaspoons baking powder
½ teaspoon salt
¼ cup shortening or margarine
1 egg, well beaten
½ cup milk
1 cup sour cream or plain yogurt

TOPPING
¼ cup brown sugar
2 tablespoons sugar
1 teaspoon cinnamon
¼ cup chopped pecans

Preheat oven to 350°F and spray a muffin pan with non-stick cooking spray. In a large bowl, mix together the flour, sugar, baking powder, and salt. Cut in the shortening until it resembles coarse crumbs. Add the egg, milk, and sour cream and stir until just moistened. In a medium bowl, combine the topping ingredients. Spoon half of the muffin batter into the muffin tins and sprinkle half of the topping evenly over the top. Spoon the remaining batter on top and sprinkle with the remaining topping. Bake 20–25 minutes, or until a toothpick inserted in the center comes away clean.

STAGECOACH INN B&B

The Stagecoach Inn was painstakingly restored in 1983 using old photos as guides. Antiques have been added to give the inn its original feeling. There are twelve comfortable guest rooms ranging from smaller rooms with queen, double, or twin-size beds, to larger rooms and suites with queen beds, in-room whirlpools, and sitting areas.

Breakfast is served daily in the pub area and includes muffins, croissants, yogurt, fruit, scones, cereal, local coffee, teas, and juice. Guests may also eat on the deck in the summer.

There is a complimentary wine and root beer social from 5–7pm in the pub where the innkeeper will show menus from local restaurants and help make reservations, as well as suggest other activities such as plays or music opportunities being presented at local theaters and the Cultural Center.

Cedar Creek Winery located at the Cedar Creek Settlement is a few blocks away, and Silvercreek Brewery is also nearby. Other area attractions include golf and tennis courts, hiking and biking trails, galleries, antique shops, a General Store Museum, a quilt store, a working blacksmith, and a number of spas.

INNKEEPERS: Brook & Liz Brown

ADDRESS: W61 N520 Washington Avenue, Cedarburg, WI 53012

TELEPHONE: (262) 375-0208; (888) 375-0208

E-MAIL: info@stagecoach-inn-wi.com

WEBSITE: www.stagecoach-inn-wi.com

ROOMS: 12 Rooms

CHILDREN: Inquire

PETS: Pet-free environment

Banana Chocolate Muffins

Makes 1 Dozen

½ cup butter
⅓ cup sugar
2 eggs
2 cups mashed bananas
1 teaspoon baking soda
1 tablespoon hot water
1½ cups all-purpose flour
¼ teaspoon salt
1 teaspoon nutmeg
½ cup chopped walnuts
½–1 cup chocolate chips

Preheat oven to 350°F and grease or line 12 muffin cups. In a large bowl, cream together the butter and sugar. Add the eggs and bananas. Dissolve the baking soda in the hot water and add to the bowl; mix well to combine. Stir in the flour, salt, nutmeg, walnuts, and chocolate chips, blending well. Fill the muffin cups about ⅔ full and bake 25 minutes.

Maple Walnut Muffins

Makes 1 Dozen

1¼ cups flour
½ teaspoon salt
1 teaspoon baking powder
½ cup firmly packed brown sugar
1 cup walnuts, chopped
1 cup sour cream
5 tablespoons butter, softened
2 eggs
½ cup maple syrup

Preheat oven to 375°F and coat 12 medium muffin cups with non-stick cooking spray. In a large bowl, combine the flour, salt, baking powder, brown sugar, and walnuts. In a separate bowl, combine the sour cream, butter, eggs, and syrup. Add the wet mixture to the flour mixture and combine. Scoop the batter into the prepared muffin cups, filling about ⅔ of the way. Bake 20–30 minutes. Let stand 10 minutes before removing from the tin.

Did you know that using sour cream in place of oil in baking will give you moister results? For a low-fat version, try yogurt in place of the sour cream.

Special Carrot-Pumpkin Mini Muffins

Makes 4 Dozen

1 box carrot cake mix
1 (15 ounce) can pumpkin
Chopped walnuts, (optional)
Dried cranberries, (optional)

Preheat oven to 350°F and spray mini-muffin cups with non-stick cooking spray. In a medium bowl, using a fork or a pastry blender, mix together the carrot cake mix and the canned pumpkin. Add in walnuts and/or cranberries for interest. Carefully scoop the batter into the prepared mini-muffin cups, filling about ¾ full. Bake 20–25 minutes and let stand 10 minutes before removing. In between batches, wipe the muffin cups clean so that you can spray additional non-stick cooking spray for the next set of muffins. Cover right away so that the muffins will stay moist while stored.

Tips and Variations

This recipe is very versatile. Use a spiced cake mix for a pumpkin pie muffin or substitute yellow butter cake mix and sprinkle a bit of cinnamon over the top. You can also add in coconut flakes or mini chocolate chips to change things up.

Red Forest B&B

Welcome to Two Rivers and the Red Forest B&B. Two Rivers is a quaint little fishing port with two meandering rivers and one Great Lake, located 35 minutes south of Green Bay.

Relax and catch a cool lake breeze at our 1907 historic b&b. Four beautifully appointed guestrooms await your arrival. We offer a full breakfast, and the aroma of early morning coffee and tea to awaken your senses.

INNKEEPERS:	Kay & Alan Rodewald
ADDRESS:	1421 25th Street, Two Rivers, WI 54241
TELEPHONE:	(920) 793-1794; (888) 250-2272
E-MAIL:	info@redforestbb.com
WEBSITE:	www.redforestbb.com
ROOMS:	4 Rooms
CHILDREN:	Inquire
PETS:	Pet-free environment

Peaches & Cream Muffins

Makes 16 Muffins

*"Our guests love these muffins! They are also
my husband's favorite so he's always looking for leftovers."*
—INNKEEPER, *Red Forest B&B*

1 (15 ounce) can peaches,
reserve juices
2 cups flour
1 cup sugar
1 teaspoon baking powder
¼ teaspoon salt
1½ eggs
⅓ cup oil
1 cup half & half

FILLING
4 ounces cream cheese, softened
⅓ cup sugar
1 tablespoon reserved
peach juice

TOPPING
¼ cup brown sugar
¼ cup sugar
1 tablespoon flour
½ teaspoon cinnamon

Preheat oven to 350°F and grease or line muffin cups. Dice the
drained peaches and set aside. In a large bowl, mix together the
flour, sugar, baking powder, and salt. In a separate bowl, combine
the eggs, oil, and half & half. Using a hand mixer, combine the
egg and flour mixtures; fold in the diced peaches. In a medium
bowl, beat together the cream cheese, sugar, and peach juice to
make the filling. Fill the muffin cups ½ full with the batter. Drop
1 teaspoon of the filling into each muffin cup and top with an
additional 1½ tablespoons of batter. Combine the topping ingredients in a small bowl and sprinkle over the muffins. Bake 20–25
minutes, until slightly browned on top. Serve warm.

Tips and Variations

Be careful not to fill the muffin cups too full with the first layer of
batter or the cream cheese filling will bubble out.

Coffee Cakes, Pastries, & Cereals

Coffee Cakes, Pastries, & Cereals

In a state known for perfecting that luscious pastry known as the Kringle, it's no wonder sweet breakfast treats reign supreme at Wisconsin B&Bs.

MILLER'S DAUGHTER B&B

Rediscover simple pleasures at the Miller's Daughter B&B in Green Lake, Wisconsin. Our celebrated lake, tranquil back roads, crystal air, and friendly small-town atmosphere combine to make Green Lake the ideal place to get away.

The Miller's Daughter was built in 1905 as a parsonage and was renovated in 2003 with up-to-date amenities to make your stay all that you had hoped for. Our guest rooms boast full private baths,

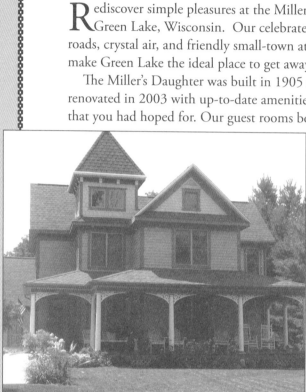

three with large whirlpool tubs and fireplaces. The inn has many unique features such as hand-painted wallpaper, stenciled ceilings, and hand painted murals. Relax on our porch, overlooking the gardens. And don't forget the full, gourmet breakfast served daily.

INNKEEPERS:	Kris & Larry Herrell
ADDRESS:	453 North Street, Green Lake, WI 54941
TELEPHONE:	920-294-0717
E-MAIL:	info@millersdaughter.com
WEBSITE:	www.millersdaughter.com
ROOMS:	5 Rooms
CHILDREN:	Facility inappropriate for children
PETS:	Pet-free environment

Rhubarb Coffee Cake

Makes 12 Servings

"I received this recipe from a neighbor 30 years ago –
the first year of our marriage. I have two patches of rhubarb
that I grow at our inn and I use this recipe every week
when the rhubarb is in season."

—INNKEEPER, *Miller's Daughter B&B*

½ cup shortening
1½ cups sugar
1 cup buttermilk*
½ teaspoon salt
2 cups flour
1 teaspoon baking soda
3 cups rhubarb, cut fine
Zest from 1 orange
½ cup chopped walnuts, (optional)

TOPPING
½ cup brown sugar
½ cup chopped walnuts
1 teaspoon cinnamon

Preheat oven to 350°F. In a large bowl, mix together the shortening, sugar, and buttermilk. In a separate bowl, sift together the salt, flour, and baking soda. Stir the dry mixture into the wet mixture until well combined. Fold in the rhubarb, orange zest, and walnuts. Pour the batter into a greased 9x13-inch baking dish. In a small bowl, combine the topping ingredients and sprinkle over the batter. Bake 35–40 minutes.

Tips and Variations

*Buttermilk substitute: 1 teaspoon baking soda, ¼ teaspoon cream of tartar, 1 cup milk

Victorian Rose B&B

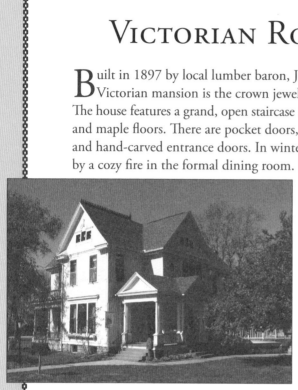

Built in 1897 by local lumber baron, John Young, this beautiful Victorian mansion is the crown jewel of Muscoda, Wisconsin. The house features a grand, open staircase and hardwood oak, walnut, and maple floors. There are pocket doors, beveled crystal windows, and hand-carved entrance doors. In winter, guests enjoy breakfast by a cozy fire in the formal dining room. In summer, the morning meal is served outside on the half-moon deck.

Muscoda is a small but vibrant community located on the Wisconsin River in beautiful Southwest Wisconsin. The area features year-round recreational opportunities such as canoeing, bicycling, snowmobiling, hunting, and fishing. There are numerous craft shows, antique galleries, and other festivals to delight you as well. The area is also a favorite with motorcycle riders who love to travel the beautiful Wisconsin River scenic byway and explore the many roads that wind through the magnificent hills.

INNKEEPERS:	Dee Davis & Dawn Miller
ADDRESS:	323 S Wisconsin Avenue, Muscoda, WI 53573
TELEPHONE:	(608) 739-4319
E-MAIL:	vrosebb@mwt.net
WEBSITE:	www.victorianrosebedandbreakfast.net
ROOMS:	3 Rooms
CHILDREN:	Facility inappropriate for children
PETS:	Pet-free environment

Cranberry Coffee Cake

Makes 1 Cake

*"This is a real crowd pleaser
and is often requested by our repeat guests."*

—INNKEEPER, *Victorian Rose B&B*

½ cup butter or margarine
1 cup sugar
2 eggs
1 cup sour cream
1 teaspoon baking soda
1 teaspoon baking powder
2 cups flour
½ teaspoon salt
¾ teaspoon almond extract
1 (16 ounce) can whole cranberry sauce
½ cup chopped nuts

FROSTING
¾ cup powered sugar
1 tablespoon warm water
½ teaspoon almond extract

Preheat oven to 350°F and grease a 9x13-inch pan. In a medium bowl, using an electric mixer, cream together the butter and sugar. Add the eggs one at a time and mix at medium speed. Reduce speed and add the dry ingredients, alternating with the sour cream. Add the almond extract. Put half of the batter in the pan and spread to the edges. Swirl half of the cranberry sauce over the mixture and top with the remaining batter. Cover with the remaining cranberry sauce and sprinkle with nuts. Bake 50 minutes. Frost while warm.

For the frosting: Mix powdered sugar with warm water and almond extract. Drizzle over the cake.

WHITE SWAN INN

White Swan Inn is a beautiful, brand new luxury b&b nestled on four and a half acres of woods only five minutes from downtown Lake Geneva. We are a romantic, country getaway, very private and cozy. All of our rooms have fireplaces, two have double whirlpools, and two have double showers.

We offer an evening wine and cheese reception and pamper our guests with early morning coffee and gourmet tea, homemade cookies, and a full, three-course, candlelit breakfast. Whether you choose the Romance Room, the Garden Room, the Seaside Room, or the Northwoods Room, our motto is "Anything your heart desires."

INNKEEPERS: Phyllis & Larry Witt

ADDRESS: W3520 Highway 50, Lake Geneva, WI 53147

TELEPHONE: (262) 348-9338

E-MAIL: innkeeper@whiteswanbb.com

WEBSITE: www.whiteswanbb.com

ROOMS: 4 Rooms

CHILDREN: Facility inappropriate for children

PETS: Resident pets

Grandma Witt's
Walnut Wonder Cake

Makes 12-16 Servings

*"This recipe was handed down from my mother-in-law Clementine.
It makes a wonderful morning coffee cake or a snack cake with coffee."*

—INNKEEPER, *White Swan Inn*

2 cups sifted flour
1 teaspoon baking powder
1 teaspoon baking soda
½ teaspoon salt
1 cup butter
1 cup sugar
2 eggs
1 teaspoon vanilla extract
1 cup sour cream

TOPPING & FILLING
⅓ cup firmly packed brown sugar
¼ cup sugar
1 teaspoon cinnamon
1 cup chopped walnuts

Preheat oven to 350°F and grease a 9 x 13-inch baking pan. Sift the flour and re-measure. Add the baking powder, baking soda, and salt and sift the entire mixture. In a separate bowl, cream together the butter and sugar until light and fluffy. Add the eggs and vanilla and beat well. Blend the sour cream and the wet mixture into the dry ingredients, beating well after each addition. Spread half of the batter in the bottom of the baking pan. In a small bowl, combine the topping ingredients. Spread half of the mixture over the batter in the pan. Smooth over the remaining batter and top with the rest of the topping. Bake 35 minutes, or until a toothpick inserted in the center comes away clean.

ANGEL INN

Innkeepers Kathy & Dave Greening purchased what was formerly a private residence in late 1999, and began renovations in January of 2000. Nine months later, renovations were complete and the first guests were welcomed to Angel Inn.

Angel Inn is a beautifully restored, turn-of-the-century Greek Revival Mansion, located on the western shores of Green Lake. Awaken each morning to spectacular sunrises over the rising mist of calm morning waters and the wafting aroma of an exquisite breakfast served in the lakefront dining room. Later, watch from the balcony as the last light of day sets ablaze the vibrant colors that surround the lake.

INNKEEPERS:	Kathy & Dave Greening
ADDRESS:	372 S Lawson Drive, Green Lake, WI 54941
TELEPHONE:	(920) 294-3087
E-MAIL:	info@angelinns.com
WEBSITE:	www.angelinns.com
ROOMS:	5 Rooms
CHILDREN:	Inquire
PETS:	Pet-free environment

Outrageous Coffee Cake

Makes 12-15 Servings

1 cup buttermilk
¼–½ cup melted butter
1 egg
1 teaspoon vanilla extract
3 cups chopped rhubarb or
　　2 cups peaches or blueberries
2¾ cups flour
1 cup sugar
1 teaspoon baking soda
½ teaspoon salt
1 cup brown sugar
½ cup chopped pecans

TOPPING
½ cup butter
½ cup cream or half & half
1 cup sugar
1 teaspoon vanilla extract

Preheat oven to 350°F and grease a 9x13-inch baking dish. In a medium bowl, mix together the buttermilk, melted butter, egg, and vanilla; stir in the fruit. In a large bowl, mix together the flour, sugar, baking soda, and salt. Stir the wet ingredients into the dry and mix until just combined. Spread the batter in the pan and sprinkle with brown sugar and pecans. Bake 45–55 minutes, or until a toothpick inserted in the center comes away clean. Stir and heat the topping ingredients in a small saucepan. When the coffee cake comes out of the oven, poke deep holes over entire surface of the cake using a meat fork or skewer. Drizzle the warm sauce over the cake, cool, and serve.

Westport B&B

Relax in our 1879 Victorian home — a blend of elegance and comfort located in Manitowoc's Historic District, near Lake Michigan, museums, trails, shops, and dining.

Each of Westport's four guest rooms features a queen bed and private bath; spa suites have whirlpools and fireplaces. Rooms also include a stocked refrigerator, flowers, snack baskets, tea table, fresh pastries, and a four-course, candlelit breakfast.

INNKEEPERS:	Janice & Paul Zencka
ADDRESS:	635 N 8th Street, Manitowoc, WI 54220
TELEPHONE:	(920) 686-0465; (888) 686-0465
E-MAIL:	stay@thewestport.com
WEBSITE:	www.thewestport.com
ROOMS:	4 Rooms
CHILDREN:	Inquire
PETS:	Pet-free environment

Blueberry Crumb Cake

Makes 10 Servings

*"This is a family recipe that we have
passed down through the years."*
—INNKEEPER, *Westport B&B*

2 cups all-purpose flour
1 cup sugar
1 tablespoon baking powder
¼ teaspoon salt
½ cup shortening
1 cup milk
2 eggs, slightly beaten
1½ cups fresh blueberries

TOPPING
1 cup sugar
½ cup flour
¼ cup melted butter

Preheat oven to 350°F and coat a 9x12-inch pan with cooking spray. Blend the flour, sugar, baking powder, and salt together in a large bowl. With a pastry blender, cut in the shortening. In a medium bowl, combine the milk and eggs and add to the dry ingredients. Mix lightly and fold in the berries. Spread the batter in the prepared pan. Combine the topping ingredients together in a small bowl and mix until crumbly; spread over the top of the batter. Bake 25 minutes, or until a toothpick inserted in the center comes away clean. Allow to cool and cut into squares to serve. A dollop of whipped cream on the side and a strawberry for garnish complete this breakfast dessert.

NAESET-ROE INN

A romantic getaway, a spot to rest from your travels, a meeting place, or a businessperson's hideaway, the Naeset-Roe Inn is all of these things. The inn is located within easy walking distance of great restaurants, art galleries and studios, live theater, pizza, a movie theater, and unique shopping.

Carl, your host and chef, has been preparing meals for almost 40 years and promises to excite your taste buds with something original for breakfast. His philosophy is, "Make it taste great, and let it have a little spark." Who says breakfast has to be bland and  sweet? Your four-course breakfast promises to keep you going for anything you have planned for the day.

So come to historic Stoughton and experience a time gone by, right here in the present. We're waiting for you.

INNKEEPER:	Carl Povlick
ADDRESS:	126 E Washington Street, Stoughton, WI 53589
TELEPHONE:	(608) 877-4150; (877) 787-5916
E-MAIL:	cpovlick@naesetroe.com
WEBSITE:	www.naesetroe.com
ROOMS:	4 Rooms
CHILDREN:	Facility inappropriate for children
PETS:	Resident pets only

Flaky Cream Scones

Makes 8-10

2 cups all-purpose flour	5½ tablespoons butter, cold
⅓ cup sugar	1 large egg, beaten
⅛ teaspoon salt	½ cup heavy cream
2 teaspoons baking powder	1 teaspoon vanilla

Preheat oven to 375°F. Place the flour, sugar, baking powder, and salt in a large mixing bowl and whisk to incorporate. Cut the butter into the flour mixture using a pastry blender, two knives, or your fingers, whatever works best for you. Cut until there are just a few large pieces of butter visible. Mix egg, vanilla, and cream together in a small bowl. Make a hole in the center of the flour and pour in the egg mixture. Fold the flour over the egg mixture with a spatula and mix gently until evenly moistened. Do not over mix. Dump the dough out onto a floured pastry cloth and knead gently 8–10 times to finish mixing. Form into a 10-inch circle about 1-inch thick. Brush the top with any egg mixture that is left on the sides of the bowl and/or 1 teaspoon cream. With a sharp straight-bladed knife, cut into 8 wedges. Place the wedges on a parchment-lined cookie sheet and bake 15 minutes. If you like them slightly darker, cook up to an additional 5 minutes or place under a broiler for a few seconds. Cool on the pan for a few minutes and then transfer to a cooling rack to cool completely. Serve with homemade flavored butters, jams, or jellies.

Tips and Variations

Try chopped cranberries, orange peel, and pecans or chopped apples, or walnuts, and brown sugar.

Remove the sugar and make them with cheddar cheese, diced ham, and onions.

Savory scones are good split and filled with scrambled or poached eggs and then finished with hollandaise or country gravy.

Pinehurst Inn
at Pike's Creek

Pinehurst Inn, an 8-room bed & breakfast located south of
Bayfield, merges the elements of the ideal lodging experience:
serene location, activities for mind and body, and soothing
amenities to rejuvenate.
The historic main
house, built in 1886,
features five guest rooms,
all designed with guests'
comfort in mind. Pine-
hurst Inn Garden House,
our "green building,"
complements the main
inn in both design and
spirit. Here you'll enjoy
three guest rooms, each
with whirlpool bath and
fireplace, and private decks. Each stay includes our heart and soul-
warming breakfast.

"Eco Friendly Elegance" —*National Geographic Traveler*

INNKEEPERS:	Nancy & Steve Sandstrom
ADDRESS:	83645 State HWY 13, Bayfield, WI 54814
TELEPHONE:	(715) 779-3676; (877) 499-7651
E-MAIL:	innkeeper@pinehurstinn.com
WEBSITE:	www.pinehurstinn.com
ROOMS:	8 Rooms
CHILDREN:	Inquire
PETS:	Resident pets only

Pinehurst Apple Lavender Scones

Makes 1 Dozen

"This recipe pulls together a mix of items from our own gardens and fruit from our local Bayfield orchards. We adapted this recipe from a basic scone recipe given to us by a friend."

—INNKEEPER, *Pinehurst Inn at Pikes Creek*

2 cups organic whole wheat pastry flour

¼ cup organic sugar

1 tablespoon baking powder

¼ teaspoon cinnamon

¼ teaspoon salt

2 teaspoons chopped lavender leaves

⅓ cup cold butter

1 cup buttermilk

1 teaspoon lemon juice

2 teaspoons lemon zest

1½ cups peeled cubed apples, or Bosc pears

Preheat oven to 375°F. Combine the flour, sugar, baking powder, cinnamon, salt, and lavender in a medium bowl. Using a pastry blender cut the cold butter (divided into 6–7 pieces) until the consistency is coarse and crumbly. Add the buttermilk, lemon juice, lemon zest, and cubed apples and stir with a fork until just moistened. If the mixture is too dry, you can add a drop or two of additional buttermilk. Knead the dough 5–6 times on a floured surface. Roll out to ¾-inch thickness and cut into preferred shapes. We use a greased scone pan to create consistent sizes. You can also drop the batter onto a greased cookie sheet lined with parchment paper. Brush the tops of the scones with egg white and sprinkle with a mixture of sugar and cinnamon. Bake 15–18 minutes, or until golden brown.

THE SCOFIELD HOUSE

Experience the welcoming warmth of a traditional and authentic bed and breakfast. At the Scofield House, a pleasing mix of old-Victorian elegance and modern conveniences combine to provide the perfect place for relaxation. Our six guestrooms are distinctly decorated, inviting intimacy and romance. Each features a fireplace,

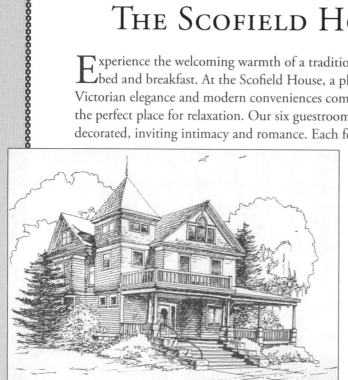

double whirlpool, fine antiques, and comfortable bed.

We serve a full breakfast in the dining room each morning. Our menu may include White Chocolate Cherry Scones, Hash-brown Breakfast Casserole, a fresh fruit course, hot coffee or tea, and a selection of juices. After a day exploring Door County, guests may return to find our Triple-Flavored Big Batch Cookies and coffee, tea, or hot chocolate.

INNKEEPERS:	Dan & Vicki Klein
ADDRESS:	908 Michigan Street, Sturgeon Bay, WI 54235
TELEPHONE:	(920) 743-7727; (888) 463-0204
E-MAIL:	stay@scofieldhouse.com
WEBSITE:	www.scofieldhouse.com
ROOMS:	6 Rooms
CHILDREN:	Facility inappropriate for children
PETS:	Pet-free environment

White Chocolate Cherry Scones

Makes 8-12 Scones

"Door County is famous for its cherries.
This is just one way to use the sweetened dried cherries
sold all over the county. Our guests love these!"
—INNKEEPER, *The Scofield House*

2 cups flour
1 tablespoon baking powder
½ teaspoon salt
¼ cup sugar
1⅓ cups cream
⅔ cup dried cherries
½ cup white chocolate chips

Preheat oven to 425°F. In a medium bowl, combine the flour, baking powder, salt, and sugar. Using a fork, stir in the cream until the dough holds together; this dough will be sticky. Fold in the cherries and white chocolate chips, mixing just until incorporated. Lightly flour a board and place the dough on it. Knead 8–9 times and then divide the dough in half. Pat and roll the dough out into two 7–8 inch diameter circles. Cut each circle into 4–6 wedges and place on ungreased cookie sheets. Sprinkle with additional sugar and bake 11–12 minutes, until golden brown on the edges.

HILL STREET B&B

We welcome you to our home and invite you to relax in one of our two living rooms filled with handcrafted woodwork, or on our front porch. We start your day with a full breakfast and always have homemade cookies and tea in the afternoon and evening.

We are conveniently located within walking distance of downtown Spring Green where you can browse through a variety of shops and art galleries. We are also close to many area attractions such as Frank Lloyd Wright's Taliesin, the American Players Theatre, and the House on the Rock. Recreational activities include championship golf, canoeing on the Wisconsin River, bicycling the county roads and trails, and hiking in the state parks.

INNKEEPER: Kelly Phelps

ADDRESS: 353 W Hill Street, Spring Green, WI 53588

TELEPHONE: (608) 588-7751

E-MAIL: hillstbb@verizon.net

WEBSITE: www.hillstreetbb.com

ROOMS: 7 Rooms; Private & shared baths

CHILDREN: Inquire

PETS: Resident pets only

Almond Date Scones

Makes 1 Dozen

1 cup all-purpose flour
1 cup whole wheat pastry flour
¼ cup brown sugar
1 tablespoon baking powder
¼ teaspoon salt
6 tablespoons unsalted butter
⅓ cup almond paste, cut into small pieces
½ cup chopped dates
1 beaten egg
½ cup half & half
½ teaspoon almond extract
¼ cup raw, coarse sugar

Preheat oven to 375°F. In a large bowl, combine the flours, brown sugar, baking powder, and salt. Cut in the butter until the mixture resembles coarse crumbs, then cut in the almond paste. Add the chopped dates and mix to combine. In a separate bowl, whisk together the egg, half & half, and almond extract, then combine with the dry ingredients. When just combined, use a medium scoop to drop the scones onto a sheet pan lined with parchment paper or a Silpat. Sprinkle with coarse sugar and bake 15 minutes, until golden brown. Turn the pan halfway through cooking. Serve warm with your favorite butter or jam.

DEER HAVEN LODGE

Deer Haven Lodge is a full log home surrounded by 218 acres of land. Soak in the tranquil beauty while getting a true taste of the great outdoors. Snowmobile and ATV trails are adjacent to our property, making for easy on/off access to the Lodge.

Wake up to a full homemade breakfast and gracious hospitality. Our deer are an attraction that entertains the nature lovers as well as hunters. The fawns are bottle fed, friendly and playful. Our 2-year-old, 14-point buck, J.R., is an awesome sight to see.

INNKEEPERS:	Ken & Lori Kiefer
ADDRESS:	16018 State HWY 13, Butternut, WI 54514
TELEPHONE:	(715) 769-3800; (715) 769-3324
E-MAIL:	lori@deerhavenlodge.net
WEBSITE:	www.deerhavenlodge.net
ROOMS:	3 Rooms
CHILDREN:	Children age 6+ older welcome; under 6 inquire
PETS:	Inquire

Mashed Potato Donuts

Makes 6-8 Servings

2 (¼ ounce) packages active-dry yeast
1½ cups warm milk
1 cup cold mashed potatoes
½ cup sugar
½ cup vegetable oil
2 teaspoons salt
2 teaspoons vanilla extract
½ teaspoon baking soda
½ teaspoon baking powder
2 eggs
5½ –6 cups all-purpose flour

In a large mixing bowl, dissolve the yeast in the warm milk. Add the potatoes, sugar, oil, salt, vanilla, baking soda, baking powder, and eggs and mix well. Add enough flour to form a soft dough. Do not knead. Place the dough in a greased bowl, turning once to grease the top. Cover and let rise in a warm place until doubled in size, about 1 hour. Punch the dough down and roll out on a floured surface to about ½-inch thickness. Cut with a 3-inch doughnut cutter and place on a greased baking sheet. Cover and let rise until almost double, about 45 minutes.

Place the doughnuts in 350°F oil and fry until golden. Glaze with a mixture of milk, vanilla extract, and powdered sugar. Enjoy!

SWEET AUTUMN INN

Sweet Autumn Inn offers three guest rooms, each with a fireplace, private bathroom, guest robes, slippers, guest refrigerator, and microwave.

No boring breakfasts here! In the morning you will enjoy a full and memorable meal. Teri easily accommodates special diets: No wheat, no eggs, no dairy, no problem! She also loves to use seasonal fruits and vegetables in her menu and grows many of them herself. From the asparagus and rhubarb in the spring to the pumpkin and apples in winter, the spicy aroma of cinnamon, cloves, nutmeg, and cardamom fill the air. Home baked breads and fresh eggs come together to make breakfast a feast. Are your taste buds tempted yet?

"The Sweet Autumn Inn offers the 'best beds' and 'best breakfasts!'"
—Guest

"Teri's personalized service and attention to detail makes your stay extra special." —Guest

INNKEEPER:	Teri Nelson
ADDRESS:	1019 S Main Street, Lake Mills, WI 53551
TELEPHONE:	(920) 648-8244; (888) 648-8244
E-MAIL:	innkeeper@sweetautumninn.com
WEBSITE:	www.sweetautumninn.com
ROOMS:	3 Rooms
CHILDREN:	Inquire
PETS:	Pet-free environment

Sweet Autumn Inn's Easy Orange Cranberry Cinnamon Rolls

Makes 10 Rolls

"I wanted to try a new Land O' Lakes recipe I'd found online, but didn't have enough orange marmalade and only one can of refrigerated biscuits. Since it was fall and cranberries are always on hand, I decided to add them to this recipe. I laid the biscuits flat over the jam and it turned out just like sticky rolls."

—INNKEEPER, *Sweet Autumn Inn*

¾ cup brown sugar
½ teaspoon cinnamon
½ cup cranberries, fresh or frozen
½ cup orange marmalade
¼ cup sugar

¼ cup chopped walnuts or pecans
1 can refrigerated flaky buttermilk biscuits
½ cup butter, melted

Preheat oven to 350°F and grease an 8 or 9-inch round baking pan. In a small bowl, stir together brown sugar and cinnamon and set aside. Place the cranberries and ¼ cup sugar together in a saucepan and cook until the berries pop and sauce thickens. Cool slightly and combine with the orange marmalade. Spoon the mixture evenly over the bottom of the baking dish and sprinkle with chopped nuts. Separate the biscuits and dip in the melted butter, then the brown sugar/cinnamon mixture. Lay the biscuits over the cranberry/marmalade. Sprinkle any remaining sugar/cinnamon mixture over the top and drizzle with any remaining butter. Bake 30–35 minutes, or until golden brown. Cool 5 minutes then invert onto a serving plate.

ESCAPE BY THE LAKE

Nestled among mature pines, Escape by the Lake spans 100 feet of beautiful Lake Mallalieu shoreline along the scenic lower St. Croix River. Located on the former site of the North Shore Resort, serenity still abounds. Our lakeshore retreat hosts the best of nature — from majestic eagles to vigorous walleye. Let Escape by the Lake's calm surroundings nurture you and soothe your soul. Bird watch

 from the deck, fish from the dock, escape on the paddle-boat, or simply bask in the year-round pleasures of the lake. Sparkling summers ease into autumn's brilliant show of changing leaves along the lakeshore followed by a peaceful blanket of white. Winter is perfect for cross-country skiing, ice fishing, or simply enjoying the view.

With just two guest rooms, you are assured VIP treatment. Choose from the Garden Room overlooking the lake and featuring Euro-lake cottage décor, or the Grand View Suite with its breathtaking view, traditional furnishings, and wood-burning fireplace: It's your choice. So whenever your travels bring you to the area, or you simply crave a retreat, come be our guests, and escape.

INNKEEPER:	Karen Langfeldt
ADDRESS:	922 Sally's Alley N, Hudson, WI 54016
TELEPHONE:	(715) 381-2871
E-MAIL:	relax@escapebythelake.com
WEBSITE:	www.escapebythelake.com
ROOMS:	2 Rooms
CHILDREN:	Inquire
PETS:	Pet-free environment

Easy Cheese Danish

Makes 8 Servings

*"I often serve this for my bread course
when I only have one room of guests – I cut the recipe in half and
bake only 18–20 minutes. Guests always rave about how wonderful
and tasty this simple recipe is. It is adapted from* California Sizzles:
Easy and Distinctive Recipes for a Vibrant Lifestyle.*"*

—INNKEEPER, *Escape by the Lake*

8 ounces cream cheese, softened
1½ teaspoons vanilla extract
¼ cup sugar
2 packages crescent roll dough
1 egg, beaten
4 ounces sliced almonds

Preheat oven to 350°F. In a medium bowl, mix together the
cream cheese, vanilla, and sugar to make the filling. Unroll 1 can
of crescents on a cookie sheet, sealing perforations. Spread the
filling on the dough, leaving a ¼-inch border around the edge.
Unroll the second can of crescent rolls and lay on top of the first
layer. Seal the edges with a fork. Brush the top with the beaten
egg and sprinkle with almonds. Bake 30 minutes, or until golden.

CLEGHORN B&B

Our guests say that Cleghorn Bed & Breakfast is so warm and friendly, it's like a "home away from home." Cleghorn is a romantic getaway and a safe, cozy place to stay while on business or pleasure.

Cleghorn is located on a wooded lot adjacent to Waupaca's beautiful Chain O' Lakes and the picturesque village of Rural, a beautiful area with lots of lakes, woods, rustic roads, and biking, hiking, and cross-country skiing paths. Each morning we serve gourmet breakfasts in a peaceful, country setting; you can enjoy the antics of the birds and wildlife right out the dining room window.

INNKEEPERS: Bob & Linda Yerkes

ADDRESS: N2080 Cleghorn Road, Waupaca, WI 54981

TELEPHONE: (715) 258-5235; (800) 870-0737

E-MAIL: info@cleghornbnb.com

WEBSITE: www.cleghornbnb.com

ROOMS: 3 Rooms

CHILDREN: Inquire

PETS: Resident pets only

Viennese Cheese Puffs

Makes 8-12 Servings

"My sister-in-law said that this is a favorite recipe in her restaurant in Oregon. Now it has become a favorite here at our b&b."
—INNKEEPER, *Cleghorn B&B*

2 packages large crescent rolls
2 (8 ounce) packages cream cheese
1 egg, separated
1 cup sugar
   (or ½ cup sugar and ½ cup Splenda)
1 teaspoon vanilla extract
⅓ cup sugar
1 teaspoon cinnamon

Preheat oven to 350°F. Press one package of crescent rolls into the bottom of a 9x13-inch pan, closing all perforations. In a medium bowl, mix together the cream cheese, egg yolk, 1 cup of sugar, and vanilla. Spread the mixture over the crescent rolls. Place the second package of rolls on waxed paper cut to the size of the pan. Seal all seams. Place over the cheese mixture (removing the waxed paper). Brush with egg white and sprinkle with a mixture of ⅓ cup sugar and cinnamon. Bake 30 minutes.

McGilvray's Victorian B&B

Come sit on my porch, relax on the swing, and let your mind drift away among comfortable surroundings. My doors are always open to you at McGilvray's Victorian Bed & Breakfast.

Call me to make a reservation for an experience that will create lasting memories.

You are invited to share the warmth, comfort, and charm that a special time and place can bring to you and your loved ones. Feel the warmth of the spacious common areas, where you can enjoy cheerful conversation and laughter. Find yourself in the comfortable surroundings of a special bedroom where you can relax and enjoy life. Explore the wonderful attractions that our beautiful city has to offer. Call us and let McGilvray's Bed & Breakfast become your home away from home. Call today and feel the warmth.

INNKEEPER: Melanie J. Berg

ADDRESS: 312 W Columbia Street, Chippewa Falls, WI 54729

TELEPHONE: (715) 720-1600; (888) 324-1893

E-MAIL: Melanie@mcgilvraysbb.com

WEBSITE: www.mcgilvraysbb.com

ROOMS: 3 Rooms

CHILDREN: Facility inappropriate for children

PETS: Pet-free environment

Farro Porridge

Makes 2 Servings

*"This is a very flavorful and hearty dish. You can also use
wild rice instead of farro if it is difficult to find in your area."*
—INNKEEPER, *McGilvray's Victorian B&B*

2 cups cooked farro
Cream
Maple syrup, to taste
2 apples, pears, or fruit of choice, in season
Fresh blueberries or cranberries
Roasted walnuts or pecans

Add enough cream to the cooked farro to make a nice creamy
consistency. Add syrup to taste. Slice, peel and core fresh fruit
of choice and sauté with butter, sugar, and cinnamon. Add fresh
blueberries or cranberries to the sautéing fruit and serve with the
farro porridge. Top with toasted walnuts or pecans.

*Farro, or emmer's wheat, is a type of
hulled wheat especially popular in
Italy. It was the first domesticated
crop in the Near East. Whole emmer
wheat can be found in many Italian
specialty markets.*

SPECKLED HEN INN

Located in Madison, Wisconsin, the Speckled Hen Inn is just 7.5 miles from the Capitol Square and University of Wisconsin campus. This b&b is the perfect place for a romantic retreat, reunion, celebration, travelers on business, or family visiting students at the university.

The 50-acre property features pastures with sheep and llamas, wetland and grassland areas, streams, pine and spruce plantations, orchards, walking trails and gardens.

Abundant, fresh, local, and seasonal describe the breakfast offerings at the Speckled Hen Inn. Start your day off right with a three-course breakfast; you choose your breakfast time. Eat early to get ahead of the crowds at The Dane County Farmers' Market, or sleep in and enjoy a leisurely breakfast at 10:00. Breakfast is served in the dining room under the big brass candelabra with real burning candles, or in the cozy library in view of the bird feeders on the back balcony.

INNKEEPERS: **Pat & Bob Fischbeck**

ADDRESS: **5525 Portage Road, Madison, WI 53704**

TELEPHONE: **(608) 244-9368; (877) 670-4844**

E-MAIL: **innkeeper@speckledheninn.com**

WEBSITE: **www.speckledheninn.com**

ROOMS: **4 Rooms**

CHILDREN: **Children age 12 and older welcome**

PETS: **Resident pets only**

Oatmeal Apple Streusel

Makes 8 Servings

*"This recipe was created to satisfy our need to serve
a bowl of oatmeal that didn't look like, well, oatmeal.
Any number of additions or substitutions can be made to the recipe
to make it seasonal or to comply with dietary restrictions. Even the
oatmeal layer could be replaced with another cooked cereal grain."*

—INNKEEPER, *Speckled Hen Inn*

APPLE LAYER

4 medium apples, peeled,
   cored and sliced

2 tablespoons butter

½ cup brown sugar

1 teaspoon cinnamon

1 tablespoon lemon juice

½ cup chopped walnuts
   or hazelnuts

OATMEAL LAYER

3 cups old-fashioned oatmeal

5 cups water (or milk or apple cider)

½ teaspoon salt

STREUSEL LAYER

½ cup flour

½ teaspoon cinnamon

¼ cup brown sugar

3 tablespoons cold butter

Lightly spray 8 5-inch round oven-proof casseroles with cooking spray. In a medium sauté pan, melt the butter and add the
sliced apples. Cook 3 minutes over medium heat and add sugar,
cinnamon, and lemon juice. Continue cooking until the sugar
has dissolved and apples are just tender. Add nuts if desired and
divide the mixture evenly between the prepared casserole dishes.
Prepare the oatmeal layer by bringing the water (or milk) to a boil
in a large saucepan. Stir in the oats and salt. Cook 5 minutes over
medium heat, stirring frequently. Remove from heat and let the
oatmeal cool while preparing the streusel layer.

Preheat oven to 350°F. In a small bowl, combine the flour, cinnamon, and brown sugar for the streusel. Using a pastry blender,
cut in the butter until it resembles very coarse crumbs. Spoon a
layer of oatmeal over the apples in the casseroles. Scatter some of
the streusel topping over each serving and bake 20–25 minutes,
or until the apple mixture is bubbling up around the edge and the
topping has browned. Serve hot.

STEWART INN

The Stewart Inn offers upscale accommodations with a gourmet breakfast in an authentic National Register Arts and Crafts masterpiece. Incredible architectural detail, modern amenities, delicious food, and unobtrusive service make for a wonderful stay.

The inn is located in downtown Wausau. Nestled around the town square are shops and restaurants, the Grand Theater, which hosts a variety of live performances, and the Center for the Visual Arts gallery and gift shop. Nearby are an excellent YMCA, the Wisconsin River Walk, and the nation's only urban whitewater kayak course. At the top of East Hill is the Woodson Art Museum, known for its annual Birds in Art exhibit. Wausau is also home to Granite Peak Ski Area, the Sylvan Hills Tubing Facility, Rib Mountain State Park, and the Wisconsin Woodchucks baseball team.

INNKEEPERS: Jane & Paul Welter

ADDRESS: 521 Grant Street, Wausau, WI 54403

TELEPHONE: (715) 849-5858

E-MAIL: innkeeper@stewartinn.com

WEBSITE: www.stewartinn.com

ROOMS: 5 Rooms

CHILDREN: Inquire

PETS: Inquire

Irish Oats with Fruit & Cranberry Syrup

Plan ahead, this dish needs to refrigerate overnight!

Makes 4 Servings

Adapted from a recipe found in *Cooking Light Magazine*.

1 cup water
1 cup milk or soy milk
1 tablespoon brown sugar
  or 1 package Splenda
¼ teaspoon cinnamon
⅛ teaspoon salt
¾ cup steel cut oats
1 can frozen cranberry juice
  concentrate

FRUIT TOPPING
¾ cup water
⅛ teaspoon salt

¼ teaspoon cinnamon
2 each dried apricots, prunes,
  and dates, chopped
¼ cup Craisins
¼ Granny Smith apple,
  peeled and chopped
2 tablespoons each raisins,
  pecans, and blueberries
½ banana, chopped
2 tablespoons cream
  or soy milk

In a saucepan over medium-high heat, combine the first five ingredients and bring to a boil. Stir in the oats, reduce heat, and continue cooking, stirring occasionally until thick, about 15 minutes. Pour into a bread pan sprayed with cooking spray. Cool to room temperature, then cover and refrigerate overnight. Thaw the cranberry juice overnight.

The following morning: Pour the juice into a saucepan and cook over medium for 20 minutes, or until juice has reduced by half and thickened. When it begins to foam, it is almost done. Set aside and it will thicken more as it cools. To prepare the fruit topping, bring the first three ingredients to a boil. Add the dried fruits, apples, and pecans to the mixture and heat 3–5 minutes, stirring gently. Add the remaining ingredients and stir just to mix. Cook one minute and set aside. Cut the chilled oats into 4 triangles. Melt 2 tablespoons butter on a non-stick skillet or griddle over medium heat. Add oat triangles and cook 3 minutes per side, or until golden brown and heated through. Put 1 triangle on a warm plate and top with ¼ cup warm fruit. Drizzle with 1–2 tablespoons of the cranberry syrup.

French Toast, Pancakes, & Waffles

French Toast, Pancakes, & Waffles

The only way to eat these is with pure
Wisconsin maple syrup. Dollops of
Wisconsin butter, fresh whipped cream,
and fruit jams are also allowed.

Brayton B&B

Brayton B&B was originally built in 1867 and fully remodeled in 2006. Just recently, the inn was named "Best Bed and Breakfast in the Great Lakes Region" by bedandbreakfast.com. A full, homemade breakfast is served each morning and desserts are offered every evening. On weekends, guests will also enjoy complimentary wine and cheese.

"What a great, relaxing place to stay! The hot breakfast each morning was delightful. One morning we had breakfast in bed — wonderful!"
—Guest

"Business travel has never felt so luxurious! Brayton B&B far exceeded my expectations. The home was absolutely beautiful and centrally located, with a wonderfully comfortable bed, handmade soaps in the shower, and sinfully delicious breakfasts. Highly recommended!"
—Guest

INNKEEPERS: Nicole & Scott Brayton
ADDRESS: 143 Church Avenue, Oshkosh, WI 54901
TELEPHONE: (920) 267-0300
E-MAIL: braytonbb@ntd.net
WEBSITE: www.braytonbb.net
ROOMS: 4 Rooms
CHILDREN: Inquire
PETS: Resident pets only

Crème Brûlée French Toast with Streusel Topping

Plan ahead, this dish needs to refrigerate overnight!

Makes 4 Servings

"This recipe is a combination of two recipes that I found in a magazine years ago and put together as one dish."

—INNKEEPER, *Brayton B&B*

1 stick butter
1 cup brown sugar
2 teaspoons corn syrup
1 loaf cinnamon bread
5 large eggs
1½ cups half & half
1 teaspoon vanilla extract

CRUMB TOPPING
¼ cup brown sugar
½ stick butter
½ teaspoon cinnamon
¼ cup chopped pecans

In a saucepan over medium-high heat, bring the butter, brown sugar, and corn syrup to a boil. Stir frequently. Pour the mixture into an 8x8-inch baking dish. Layer the bread over the glaze, 2–4 slices high, making them fit the pan. In a medium bowl, whisk together the eggs, half & half, and vanilla until combined. Pour over the bread, cover, and chill overnight.

The following morning: Preheat oven to 500°F. Bake, uncovered, for 15 minutes. In a small bowl, mix together the crumb topping; sprinkle over the baked French toast. Bake an additional 10 minutes. Serve with strawberry jam.

THE FRINGE, A COUNTRY INN

The Fringe is perfect for both business travelers and vacationers alike. This 1922 country farm home is designed for comfort and relaxation. Each of the four beautiful and spacious rooms comes complete with sitting area, private deluxe whirlpool baths, and refrigerators with complimentary water and soft drinks. Each morning guests will enjoy a home-style breakfast that starts with

bread, then fresh fruit, and the main dish. Other amenities include in-house massages and gift baskets by Perfect Touch Baskets.

The inn is conveniently located close to many Sheboygan area recreational activities and events including Lake Michigan, Kohler Design Center, Woodlake Market, and Road America. World-class golf is only minutes away; choose from either The Bull at Pinehurst Farms, Blackwolf Run, or Whistling Straits, site of the 2004 PGA Championship.

"Beautiful place, excellent food and hospitality." —GUEST

"Awesome breakfast and we really enjoyed the whirlpool tub." —GUEST

INNKEEPERS:	Ruth & Carl Paul
ADDRESS:	711 Giddings Avenue, Sheboygan Falls, WI 53085
TELEPHONE:	(920) 467-3172; (866) 374-6430
E-MAIL:	info@thefringecountryinn.com
WEBSITE:	www.thefringecountryinn.com
ROOMS:	4 Rooms
CHILDREN:	Inquire
PETS:	Pet-free environment

Berries 'N' Cream French Toast

Makes 8 Servings

*"We like to serve this recipe to wedding couples
that choose to remain in their room the morning after their wedding.
It also works well for a larger group: simply use a large griddle."*

—INNKEEPER, *The Fringe, A Country Inn*

6 ounces cream cheese, softened
½ cup marshmallow creme
½ teaspoon vanilla extract
2 cups sliced fresh or frozen strawberries
¼ cup sugar
1½ teaspoons cornstarch
1 tablespoon cold water
3 eggs
¾ cup milk
8 slices Texas toast

In a small mixing bowl, beat the cream cheese, marshmallow
creme, and vanilla until smooth; set aside. In a small saucepan,
bring the strawberries and sugar to a boil. Reduce heat and simmer, uncovered, for 10 minutes. Combine the cornstarch and
cold water and mix until smooth; stir into the berry mixture.
Return to a boil and cook, stirring constantly, for 2 minutes,
or until thickened. Remove from heat; keep warm.

In a shallow bowl, whisk together the eggs and milk. Dip both
sides of the bread in the egg mixture. Cook the bread on a lightly
greased, hot skillet over medium heat, two minutes per side, or
until golden brown. To serve, spread each piece of Texas toast
with the cream cheese mixture. Top with the strawberry syrup
and garnish with whole strawberries.

Lighthaus Inn B&B

Enjoy our country getaway located on a private road overlooking the valley. Watch the sunset from the tower balcony of our full-size lighthouse. The private Guesthaus, with full kitchen and living quarters, offers a cozy furnished respite.

Our country estate features large yards, fishponds, and lots to see. Make your vacation to the Coulee Region a weeklong stay at

our home and you will never run out things to do. Enjoy great bike trails, complete with train tunnels, or visit the Amish communities for a look back into time.

Come see.

Come stay.

Come back…

INNKEEPERS:	Kristen & Reinhard Mueller
ADDRESS:	9529 Gardener Avenue, Sparta, WI 54656
TELEPHONE:	(608) 269-4002; (888) 277-1001
E-MAIL:	info@lighthausinn.com
WEBSITE:	www.lighthausinn.com
ROOMS:	1 Guesthaus
CHILDREN:	Welcome
PETS:	Inquire

French Toast Surprise

Plan ahead, this dish needs to refrigerate overnight!

Makes 8 Servings

*"My extended family gathers for holidays at my grandpa's farm.
This baked French toast is just one of the many items that is on
the table. My Aunt Carla makes it regularly, with Uncle Dan
frying eggs to order. I have made some changes to make it
more versatile for the seasons."*

—INNKEEPER, *Lighthaus Inn B&B*

8 eggs	FRUIT GLAZE
1½ cups cream	½ cup melted butter
1 tablespoon brown sugar	½ cup maple syrup
2 tablespoons vanilla extract	¾ cup brown sugar
8–12 slices heavy bread	½ cup chopped pecans
	1 (21 ounce) can pie filling fruit, peaches, apples, or pineapple

In a large bowl, mix together the eggs, cream, brown sugar, and
vanilla. Soak the bread in the mixture while your oven preheats to
350°F. In a 9x13-inch pan, mix together the melted butter, syrup,
brown sugar, pecans, and fruit. When in doubt, add more brown
sugar and use only real maple syrup. You can vary the nuts and
the fruit; whatever you have on hand will work. Lay the soaked
bread on top of the mixture and bake 30 minutes, until puffy and
brown. Sprinkle lightly with powdered sugar.

To serve: spoon a portion of the French toast onto a serving plate,
making sure to top with some of the "good stuff" from the pan.
Serve with wild rice, sausage, or glazed ham.

Tips and Variations

The recipe calls for soaking the bread in the egg mixture overnight, however, it can be soaked in the morning while the other
ingredients are being prepared.

THE ROSE OF SHARON B&B

The Rose of Sharon Bed and Breakfast was originally built by Philip and Minnie Lingelbach in the early 1900s. Philip was the brewmeister for the Oconto Brewery, which was located next to the house. One of our guest rooms is dedicated to them, and is

graced with family photos and a claw-foot tub where Mrs. Lingelbach once enjoyed her bubble baths.

Our home has the largest wrap-around porch in town and guests enjoy sitting on the porch swing and sipping iced tea or coffee. At breakfast we often have guests tell us how comfortable the bed is in Amri's Garden room. Hope you'll join us soon and find out for yourself.

INNKEEPERS:	Thomas & Irma Majors
ADDRESS:	1109 Superior Avenue, Oconto, WI 54153
TELEPHONE:	(920) 737-6650
E-MAIL:	rose_bnb@yahoo.com
WEBSITE:	www.roseofsharonbnb.net
ROOMS:	3 Rooms
CHILDREN:	Inquire
PETS:	Pet-free environment

Apple Caramel Stuffed French Toast

Makes 4-6 Servings

4 ounces cream cheese, softened*
1 medium apple, peeled and chopped
2 tablespoons caramel topping
¼ cup chopped walnuts or pecans
8–12 pieces soft white bread
2–3 eggs, beaten
Cinnamon
2 tablespoons milk

In a medium, microwave-safe bowl, heat the cream cheese until soft, about 20 seconds. Remove and add the chopped apple, caramel topping, and nuts. Mix thoroughly with a spoon. Spread the apple mixture over the center of one piece of bread (the size of a round crimper or biscuit cutter). Top with a second piece of bread and use the crimper to cut out individual rounds. In a medium bowl, mix together the eggs, cinnamon, and milk. Heat then spray a griddle with non-stick cooking spray. Dip each round sandwich in the egg mixture and place on the heated griddle. Brown on one side, flip and brown on the other. Cover the cooked French toast with foil and place in a warm oven until ready to serve.

To serve: Place the French toast on a plate and sprinkle with powdered sugar and nuts. Serve with butter and syrup.

Tips and Variations

*For low-fat version, try substituting 6–8 ounces plain or vanilla yogurt.

RIVERVIEW B&B

Riverview is located by the White River in Neshkoro, a quiet little fishing village that offers the joys of solitude and the jollity of nearby attractions. Visit the area bison farm, Prairie Nursery farm and flea markets, Ice Age and Rustic Road trails. In the summer, tube the White River, and visit the beach. In the winter enjoy cross-country skiing, and snowmobile trails. You can also drive to the EAA Museum, Wisconsin Dells, or even Lambeau Field, then return to rest here.

"As I am sitting in my favorite rocking chair and looking onto the lovely porch, I do not have the words to describe the emotions I have felt staying in your home. My first b&b experience was perfect. Your touch was warm, your home was cozy and your windows glowed with the light from your soul. Thank you for everything and more."

—GUEST

INNKEEPER:	Marilyn Brockopp
ADDRESS:	219 W Wall Street, Neshkoro, WI 54960
TELEPHONE:	(920) 293-4423
E-MAIL:	rivervu_marilyn@charter.net
WEBSITE:	www.theriverviewbnb.com
ROOMS:	3 Rooms
CHILDREN:	Inquire
PETS:	Pet-free environment

Apples & Cinnamon Deep-Dish Toast

Makes 8 Servings

4 eggs, slightly beaten

1 cup milk

1 teaspoon vanilla extract

¼ teaspoon baking powder

1 loaf French bread, cut into 1-inch slices

2 large cooking apples,
     peeled, cored, and thinly sliced

½ cup brown sugar

1 teaspoon cinnamon

2 tablespoons butter, melted

Preheat oven to 450°F and spray one 9x13-inch baking dish with non-stick cooking spray. In a large bowl, whisk together the eggs, milk, vanilla, and baking powder. Place the bread slices in a separate, ungreased 9x13-inch baking dish and pour the egg mixture over the bread. Turn to coat then cover the pan with plastic wrap and let stand until all of the liquid is absorbed. Add another egg and more milk to make additional custard if you like. Place the apples in a layer on the bottom of the greased pan and sprinkle with brown sugar and cinnamon. Arrange the soaked bread slices over the top of the apples and brush with melted butter. Bake in the center of preheated oven for 25 minutes, or until golden brown. Serve with maple syrup and whipped cream or dust with powdered sugar.

Tips and Variations

For preparation the night before, place the dish with the soaking bread slices in the refrigerator overnight. The following morning remove from the fridge and follow remaining directions. Serve with bacon, juice, coffee, or whatever else you choose.

Trollhaugen Lodge

O ur bed and breakfast inn has the homey feel of a guesthouse. Uniquely decorated rooms with queen beds are romantic, cozy retreats for adults only. Choose a first-floor room with or without a wood-burning fireplace, a second-floor room with a balcony, or our second-floor mini-suite featuring a king poster bed, a double sofa sleeper, gas fireplace, entertainment center, refrigerator, microwave, coffeemaker, wet bar, and a private deck with table and chairs.

Our guests enjoy a hot and cold breakfast buffet and afternoon treats.

Walk to the waterfront for sunsets and the center of town for shopping and dining, enjoy our nearby hiking trail, or relax in our outdoor whirlpool.

INNKEEPERS: Norma & Terry Street
ADDRESS: 10176 HWY 42, Ephraim, WI 54211
TELEPHONE: (920) 854-2713; (800) 854-4118
E-MAIL: trollhaugen@dcwis.com
WEBSITE: www.trollhaugenlodge.com
ROOMS: 5 Rooms
CHILDREN: Facility inappropriate for children
PETS: Pet-free environment

Breakfast Lasagna

Makes 8-12 Servings

PASTRY CREAM

1 cup sugar

½ cup all-purpose flour

½ teaspoon salt

2 cups milk

9 egg yolks

2 teaspoons vanilla extract

FRUIT LAYER

1 pint strawberries

1 cup blueberries

1 cup fresh peaches

3 bananas, sliced

1 tablespoon butter to grease pan

PANCAKES

1½ cups sifted flour

2½ teaspoons baking powder

¾ teaspoon salt

1 egg, well beaten

1¼ cups milk

3 tablespoons shortening, melted and slightly cooled, or salad oil

For the pastry cream: In a 2-quart saucepan over medium heat, whisk together sugar, flour, salt, and milk. Cook the mixture until it thickens. In a small bowl, beat the egg yolks slightly. Using a fork, beat in a small amount of the milk mixture. Slowly pour the egg mixture into the milk mixture. Stirring constantly, cook over medium-low heat until the mixture thickens. Remove from heat and stir in the vanilla. Chill in the refrigerator until ready to use. You will need a total of 2½ cups of pastry cream for this recipe.

For the pancakes: Sift together the flour, baking powder, and salt. In a medium bowl, mix together the egg, milk, and shortening. Pour the milk mixture into the dry ingredients and stir until just moistened. Cook on a hot, lightly greased skillet, turning pancakes only once. You will need 12 pancakes for this recipe.

To assemble: Preheat oven to 350°F. Put a thin layer of pastry cream in a buttered 13x9-inch pan. Top with a layer of pancakes then another layer of pastry cream. Slice the strawberries in half. Layer half of the strawberries, blueberries, peaches, and bananas in the pan to make a layer of fruit. Top the fruit with a layer of pancakes, then layer the rest of the fruit on top. Bake for 20 minutes.

COBBLESTONE B&B

Cobblestone Bed and Breakfast is designed around the concept of simple comfort and elegance. Take a step back in time as you sip tea and relax on the front porch swing. Enjoy an elegant breakfast next to a crackling fire on a wintry morn. Take a piece of the Northwoods home after browsing through ye old gift shoppe.

Much thought has been taken to leave the house in its original state while updating to add private baths, fireplaces, and other amenities. Cobblestone's most popular room is the English Garden Suite, which offers a king-size bed and whirlpool tub for two imported from France. A close second is the Love at First Site room with its copper and nickel soaking tub.

INNKEEPER:	Mary Lou Campion
ADDRESS:	319 S Main Street, Birchwood, WI 54817
TELEPHONE:	(715) 354-3494
E-MAIL:	cobblestone@centurytel.net
WEBSITE:	www.cobblestonebedandbreakfast.com
ROOMS:	5 Rooms; Private & shared baths
CHILDREN:	Welcome
PETS:	Inquire

Buttermilk Pancakes

Makes 4-6 Servings

Have to give credit to Jenny on this one!"

—INNKEEPER, *Cobblestone B&B*

1 egg
1½ cups flour
1 tablespoon sugar
¾ teaspoon salt
1¾ teaspoons baking powder
1 teaspoon baking soda
2 cups buttermilk
2½ tablespoons margarine or oil

Separate the egg and beat the white until fluffy peaks form. In a separate bowl, mix together the egg yolk, flour, sugar, salt, baking powder, baking soda, buttermilk, and margarine. When the batter is well mixed, fold (do not stir) in the beaten egg white. Cook ¼ cup of the batter in a heated skillet over medium heat until bubbles appear. Flip and cook other side. Repeat until all of the batter has been used.

Tips and Variations

Try adding fresh berries, chocolate chips, or nuts to the batter for special occasion pancakes. Chopped bananas and pecans are a great combination as well.

INN ON MAPLE

Inn on Maple is a charming Historic Register home with six upstairs guest rooms, each featuring antique armoires and queen-sized beds with wonderful fresh linens. The inn also has a separate room with two twin beds, great for visiting families. Watch a movie,

play a game, or curl up with a book by the fire in the comfortable Gathering Room. Spend the afternoon relaxing on the backyard deck as you watch the birds fly by.

Each morning you'll enjoy a delightful full breakfast that includes fresh fruit, homemade muffins or bread, a daily entrée, juice, coffee, and tea. Breakfast is served on the enclosed front porch, or outdoors on the deck, weather permitting. Afternoon cookies and beverages are also served daily.

INNKEEPERS: Bill & Louise Robbins

ADDRESS: 2378 Maple Drive, Sister Bay, WI 54234

TELEPHONE: (920) 854-5107

E-MAIL: innonmaple@dcwis.com

WEBSITE: www.innonmaple.com

ROOMS: 6 Rooms

CHILDREN: Facility inappropriate for children

PETS: Resident pets only

Buttermilk Pancakes with Apple Tatin

Makes 8 Servings

*"Our guests enjoy this special pancake dish,
especially in the fall when we serve the Apple Tatin portion
cut in the shape of maple leaves! We offer Door County
maple syrup and apple smoked bacon or sausage for added taste."*
—INNKEEPER, *Inn on Maple*

2 cups flour
2 teaspoons sugar
2 heaping teaspoons
  baking powder
1 teaspoon baking soda
1 teaspoon salt
2 eggs
2 cups buttermilk
¼ cup vegetable oil

APPLE TATIN
1 9-inch round puff pastry
3 tablespoons softened,
  unsalted butter, cut into bits
2 Granny Smith apples,
  peeled, cored, and sliced thin
1 teaspoon grated lemon peel
1 tablespoon lemon juice,
  or to taste
¼ cup sugar
Sifted confectioners' sugar, to taste

In a medium bowl, combine the flour, sugar, baking powder, baking soda, and salt; mix well. In a separate bowl, combine the eggs, buttermilk, and oil and mix well. Add the wet mixture to the dry ingredients and stir until moist, but slightly lumpy. Do not over mix. Pour ¼ cup of the batter onto a hot, lightly greased griddle and bake until brown on both sides. Continue until all the batter has been used. Serve layered with slices of apple tatin, sprinkle with confectioners' sugar, and drizzle with maple syrup.

For the apple tatin: Preheat oven to 425°F. Using the tines of a fork, lightly prick the puff pastry. Butter a cookie sheet and arrange the pastry. Spread 1 tablespoon of the butter over the pastry. In a bowl, toss the apple slices with the lemon peel and lemon juice. Arrange the apple slices in one layer on the pastry in a circle, over-lapping slightly. Sprinkle with the sugar and dot with the remaining butter. Bake 20–25 minutes, or until golden brown.

Hazelhurst Inn

Whether you are looking for rest, relaxation, a midweek break, or a weeklong retreat, the Hazelhurst Inn is an ideal vacation location. The inn is adjacent to the Bearskin State Trail, an old railroad bed with a crushed granite base that's great for hiking, biking, bird watching, and wildlife viewing. Hazelhurst is also just five miles south of Minocqua and its many gift shops, antique malls, clothing stores, and fine restaurants.

The Northwoods area is known for its lakes and water sports. Guests should take advantage of the great fishing, boating, skiing, and even lounging at the shore. Winter sports are also abundant in northern Wisconsin. Enjoy cross country skiing, ice fishing, snow shoeing, and snowmobiling — the Bearskin Trail is a snowmobile trail in the winter.

INNKEEPERS:	Sharon Goetsch
ADDRESS:	6941 State Highway 51, Hazelhurst, WI 54531
TELEPHONE:	(715) 356-6571
E-MAIL:	hzhrstbb@newnorth.net
WEBSITE:	www.hazelhurstinn.com
ROOMS:	4 Rooms
CHILDREN:	Welcome
PETS:	Welcome

Orange Thyme Pancakes with Orange Glaze

Makes 5-6 Servings

2 cups flour
1 teaspoon salt
2 teaspoons baking soda
¼ cup sugar
½ teaspoon thyme
2 eggs, beaten
1¾ cups orange juice
½ stick butter, melted

ORANGE GLAZE
1 stick butter
3 tablespoons cornstarch
⅔ cup sugar
2 cups orange juice, heated
1 teaspoon orange zest
¼ teaspoon thyme

Mix together the flour, salt, baking soda, sugar, and thyme. Add the eggs and stir to combine. Mix in the juice and the butter. Pour ¼ cup of the batter onto a 350°F heated griddle to make each pancake.

For the glaze: Melt the butter in a medium saucepan over medium-high heat. Mix in the cornstarch to make a white roux. Stir in the heated orange juice and the remaining glaze ingredients. Drizzle hot sauce over the pancakes.

THE ATRIUM B&B

The Atrium, nestled on fifteen wooded acres, is named for one of its many impressive features: the conservatory room at the heart of the home. A palm and fig tree stretch upward toward a windowed twenty-foot ceiling, and bougainvillea vines encircle the reading loft above. The contemporary home boasts magnificent antique stained-glass windows.

Wake to the aroma of fresh-brewed coffee on a "wake-up tray" delivered to your door. Enjoy fresh-baked breads while we prepare

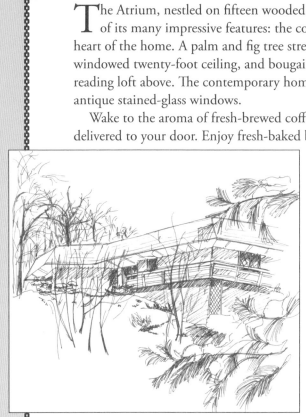

your delectable three-course breakfast, served to you in the dining room, atrium, or on a tray in your room. Our menu changes daily to take advantage of our fresh Chippewa Valley grown fruits, Wisconsin cheeses, herbs from our garden, and locally acclaimed breakfast sausages.

INNKEEPERS: **Celia & Dick Stoltz**
ADDRESS: **5572 Prill Road, Eau Claire, WI 54701**
TELEPHONE: **(715) 833-9045; (888) 773-0094**
E-MAIL: **info@atriumbb.com**
WEBSITE: **www.atriumbb.com**
ROOMS: **4 Rooms**
CHILDREN: **Children age 12 and older welcome**
PETS: **Pet-free environment**

Gingerbread Pancakes with Warm Lemon Sauce

Makes 10 Thin Pancakes

'These are tender, light, and so delicious with the 'must serve' warm lemon sauce."
—INNKEEPER, *The Atrium B&B*

1½ cups all-purpose flour	LEMON SAUCE
1 teaspoon baking powder	½ cup sugar
1 teaspoon cinnamon	4 teaspoons cornstarch
½ teaspoon ginger	1 cup water
¼ baking soda	2 tablespoons butter
¼ teaspoon salt	2 tablespoons lemon juice
1 egg	½ teaspoon lemon zest
1½ cups milk	
¼ cup molasses	
3 tablespoons cooking oil	

In a medium mixing bowl, whisk together the flour, baking powder, cinnamon, ginger, baking soda, and salt. In a large mixing bowl, beat together the egg and milk until combined. Add in the molasses and oil and beat until incorporated. Add the dry ingredients to the liquid mixture and stir just until blended. The batter should be slightly lumpy and thin. Pour ¼ cup of the batter onto a heated griddle and cook until the edges are dry and the pancake surface is bubbly. Turn and cook another minute or so, until done. Pancakes should be thin. Dust with powdered sugar and serve immediately with warm lemon sauce.

For the sauce: In a small saucepan over medium heat, combine the sugar and cornstarch; stir in the water. Cook and stir over medium heat until the mixture become thick and bubbly. Cook and stir an additional 2 minutes. Remove from heat and add the butter, lemon juice, and lemon zest. Serve warm with gingerbread pancakes.

BOWMAN'S OAK HILL B&B

From the spacious romantic bedrooms, lovely bathrooms, and the yummy breakfast served in our dining area or on our large deck, to the eight acres of park-like setting and 25 acres of woods to wander, you will have the opportunity to rest, reflect, relax and be renewed both in body and spirit during your stay with us here at Oak Hill.

Bowman's Oak Hill is just a brief 5-minute drive from the center of the Wisconsin Dells River District. Innkeepers David and Nancy are happy to help guests with their plans for a memorable stay. Nearby attractions include the new Broadway Dinner Theater, Crystal Grand Music Theater, the Rick Wilcox Magic Theater, casual and fine dining, river boat tours, the Tommy Bartlet Water Ski show, both indoor and outdoor water parks, horseback riding, and golfing.

INNKEEPERS:	David & Nancy Bowman
ADDRESS:	4169 State HWY 13, Wisconsin Dells, WI 53965
TELEPHONE:	(888) 253-5631
E-MAIL:	bowmansoakhillbb@aol.com
WEBSITE:	www.bowmansoakhillbedandbreakfast.com
ROOMS:	3 Rooms; 2 Cottages
CHILDREN:	Inquire
PETS:	Resident pets only

Nancy's Gourmet Pancakes

Makes 12 Pancakes

"I got this recipe from a neighbor on the 4th of July, 45 years ago, when I was a very young mother. From that day forward, my girls did not think pancakes were truly pancakes without this sauce."

—INNKEEPER, *Bowman's Oak Hill B&B*

1¼ cups flour	1 cup light cottage cheese
⅓ cup sugar or sugar substitute	½ cup plain yogurt
1 teaspoon baking soda	½ cup light sour cream
½ teaspoon baking powder	1 teaspoon vanilla extract
Dash of salt	2 eggs

In a large bowl, combine the flour, sugar, baking soda, baking powder, and salt. In a second bowl, combine the cottage cheese, yogurt, sour cream, vanilla, and eggs. Heat a griddle to medium. Once heated, combine the wet and dry mixtures. Butter or spray the griddle with non-stick cooking spray. Place 1/4 cup of batter on the griddle, the batter will be thick. Turn when the top bubbles and the edges begin to dry. It will take about 3 minutes per side to cook. Continue until all the batter has been used.

We serve these with lemon sauce and fresh raspberries from our garden, when in season. We also offer real maple syrup as another option.

Nancy's Secret Lemon Sauce

Makes 1½ Cups

1 egg, beaten	¼ cup water
1 cup sugar	½ cup butter
Zest of 1 lemon	Dash of salt
Juice of 1 lemon, or ¼ cup bottled lemon juice	

Place all of the ingredients in a medium saucepan, over medium-high heat, stirring occasionally. Bring just to a boil before pouring into a small pitcher. Serve with warm pancakes.

ANNIE'S GARDEN

All to yourselves...total seclusion...You are the only guests at Annie's! Enjoy peace and seclusion at Madison's most uncommon lodging.

Surrounded by trees and lush gardens, Annie's is nestled alongside a beautiful wooded vista of south Warner Park, near the eastern shore of Lake Mendota. Stroll the lakeshore at sunset and explore the marshes and woods to catch a glimpse of deer, fox, and countless birds.

The rustic cedar shake house is a gem; owner-designed in the 1960's and chock-full of fascinating original art reflecting a deep appreciation of nature. The suite includes a pine-paneled library with lannon stone fireplace, a perfect place to read and listen to music. There is also a master bedroom, a smaller bedroom, and full bath. On the lower level, enjoy a double Jacuzzi or view movies from Annie's extensive collection in the DVD theater, complete with popcorn, all for you alone.

INNKEEPERS:	Annie & Larry Stuart
ADDRESS:	2117 Sheridan Drive, Madison, WI 53704
TELEPHONE:	(608) 244-2224
E-MAIL:	innkeeper@anniesinmadison.com
WEBSITE:	www.anniesinmadison.com
ROOMS:	1 Full suite
CHILDREN:	Inquire
PETS:	Resident pets only

ANNIE'S
BREAKFAST COOKIES

Makes 2 Dozen

3½ cups milk

6 tablespoons vegetable oil

6 large eggs, beaten

1 cup raisins

4 cups old-fashioned oats

4 tablespoons brown sugar

1 tablespoon baking powder

½ teaspoon salt

1½ cups chopped fruit of choice
   (apples, cranberries, or bananas)

1 cup chopped nuts

In a large bowl, combine the milk, oil, beaten eggs, and raisins. Add the oats and soak for five minutes. Stir in the brown sugar, baking powder, and salt. Fold in the fruit and nuts. Spread ¼ cup of the batter on an oiled griddle set to no more than 325°F. Turn once, do not allow it to brown but rather to just cook through. Continue until all the batter has been used.

Tips and Variations

These pancakes will be thick and hearty. Serve with maple syrup, fresh fruit, a generous heap of country bacon or sausages, and a tall, frosty glass of fresh orange juice

COUNTRY COMFORT

Country Comfort, a Bed & Breakfast, is that special place created for your rest and relaxation — your home away from home! Enjoy a very comfortable night's sleep in one of our four spacious guest rooms, and wake to the smell of great coffee and a scrumptious and plentiful breakfast. Legacy Chocolate and complimentary wine in the evening are guaranteed to make your stay blissful.

While in Menomonie, take time to enjoy area attractions such as the Red Cedar Trail, Mabel Tainter Memorial Theater, Wilson Place Museum, Rassbach Heritage Museum, Lions Club Game

Park, University of Wisconsin–Stout, Caddie Woodlawn Museum and Park, Hoffman Hills Hiking Trails, antique shops, art galleries, golf courses, fishing, snowmobile trails, and fabulous cuisine.

INNKEEPERS:	Loren & Judy Gifford
ADDRESS:	N5126 410th Street, Menomonie, WI 54751
TELEPHONE:	(715) 233-0113
E-MAIL:	info@staycountrycomfort.com
WEBSITE:	www.staycountrycomfort.com
ROOMS:	4 Rooms
CHILDREN:	Facility inappropriate for children
PETS:	Pet-free environment

Pumpkin Pecan Pancakes

Makes 4 Servings

1 cup pastry flour
¼ cup sugar
1 teaspoon cinnamon
$\frac{1}{16}$ teaspoon cloves
$\frac{1}{8}$ teaspoon nutmeg
$\frac{1}{16}$ teaspoon allspice
¼ teaspoon salt
½ teaspoon baking powder
1 cup pumpkin purée
2 eggs
1 cup half & half
2 ounces melted butter
4 egg whites, whipped to soft peaks

2 tablespoons vegetable oil
1 cup chopped pecans,
 slightly roasted

CARAMEL SAUCE
½ cup water
1 cup sugar
1 cup heavy cream
¼ teaspoon table salt
¾ teaspoon vanilla extract
½ teaspoon lemon juice

Sift together all of the dry ingredients. In a bowl, combine the purée, whole eggs, and half & half. Add the flour mixture and stir, being careful not to over mix the batter. Add in the melted butter and then fold in half of the egg whites. When they are nearly incorporated, fold in the rest of the eggs whites. Gently fold in pecans. The trick is not to over mix the batter, you want to leave plenty of white streaks. Heat a griddle to medium and drizzle with enough vegetable oil to prevent sticking. Spoon the batter onto the griddle, spreading with the back of the spoon. When the pancakes are golden brown, flip to finish cooking. Serve with caramel sauce.

For the caramel sauce: Place the water in a heavy-bottomed 2-quart saucepan and pour the sugar into the center of the pan. Make sure not to let the sugar stick to the sides of the pan. Cover and bring to a boil. Uncover and boil until the syrup is thick and straw colored (300°F on a candy thermometer), about 7 minutes. Reduce heat and continue to cook until it reaches 350°F. In a separate pan, bring the cream and salt to a simmer over high heat. If the mixture boils before the sugar is done, remove from heat and cover to keep warm. Remove the sugar syrup from heat and very carefully pour ¼ of the cream into it. Let the bubbling subside before adding the remaining cream, vanilla, and lemon. Whisk until smooth.

THE ARTESIAN HOUSE

The Artesian House, the vision of Margaret Rdzak and Al Chechik, opened in June 1996. Sadly, Margaret enjoyed the fulfillment of her dream only briefly, and succumbed to cancer that October. Today, the inn reflects a creative mix of the contemporary and the eclectic, and is comfortably secluded on 24 acres close to Bayfield and Lake Superior. Its walking trail features lupines in June and berries and apples in summer and fall. There are four individually themed guest rooms, a great room with floor-to-ceiling windows, a rain garden, and a newly added solar installation for hot water.

"[The Artesian House is] a wonderful experience with a most congenial host, gorgeous rooms, spectacular architecture, and sumptuous breakfasts."

—GUEST

INNKEEPER:	Al Chechik
ADDRESS:	84100 Hatchery Road, Bayfield, WI 54814
TELEPHONE:	(715) 779-3338
E-MAIL:	artesian@ncis.net
WEBSITE:	www.artesianhouse.com
ROOMS:	4 Rooms
CHILDREN:	Welcome
PETS:	Pet-free environment

Dutch Baby Oven Pancake

Makes 6-8 Servings

"Twin Cities guests recognize this as a panekuchen,
still offered at a popular Minneapolis restaurant."
—INNKEEPER, *The Artesian House*

3 large eggs
¾ cup milk
¾ cup flour
¼ cup butter

Preheat oven to 425°F. In a medium bowl, beat the eggs, add in the milk and gradually beat in the flour; mix well. Melt the butter in a 2–3 quart cast-iron skillet, on the stovetop. Pour the batter into the skillet and place in the heated oven. Bake 28–30 minutes, until puffy and evenly browned.

To serve: Cut into wedges. For breakfast, serve with fresh fruit, yogurt, syrup, and powdered sugar. For dessert, serve with ice cream, whipped cream, chocolate sauce, and cherries. Use your imagination; it's great with everything!

CAMEO ROSE
VICTORIAN COUNTRY INN

Nestled amid 120 acres of rolling hills and scenic woodlands is the Cameo Rose, a peaceful retreat just minutes from Madison, New Glarus, and many charming historic communities.

Situated near four state bike trails, this park-like estate, enhanced with miles of meandering groomed hiking trails, is teeming with birds, deer, and other wildlife. Victorian gardens, gazebos, and pergolas display a profusion of roses and flowers surrounding the

hanging swings, seating areas, and hammocks tucked inside. The pond with its three impressive waterfalls also features a 16-foot screened gazebo, strategically placed to offer a panoramic view of the rocky outcroppings on the majestic hillside beyond.

INNKEEPERS:	Dawn & Gary Bahr
ADDRESS:	1090 Severson Road, Belleville, WI 53508
TELEPHONE:	(608) 424-6340; (866) 424-6340
E-MAIL:	innkeeper@cameorose.com
WEBSITE:	www.cameorose.com
ROOMS:	5 Rooms
CHILDREN:	Children age 12 and older welcome
PETS:	Pet-free environment

Deep Dish Apple Berry Pancake

Makes 6-8 Servings

*"We have an abundance of wild, organic berries on our property
that I pick and freeze to include in this recipe as well as
our signature triple berry stuffed French toast and buttermilk
muffins, or just to serve fresh with our fruit course.
Guests are welcome to nibble on the raspberries and blackberries
as they explore our rambling, groomed nature trails."*

—INNKEEPER, *Cameo Rose Victorian Country Inn*

1 stick butter	⅓ cup sugar
6 extra large eggs	¼ teaspoon salt
1½ cups milk	6 large apples, sliced
1 teaspoon vanilla extract	1 teaspoon allspice
½ teaspoon maple extract	1 teaspoon pumpkin pie spice
1 teaspoon plus	½ cup each: whole cranberries,
1 tablespoon cinnamon, divided	blackberries, and raspberries
⅛ teaspoon plus	(fresh or frozen)
¼ teaspoon nutmeg, divided	½ cup coarsely chopped pecans
1 cup flour	½ cup packed brown sugar

Heat oven to 425°F. Spray the bottom and sides of a 9x13-inch
baking dish with non-stick cooking spray or shortening. Cut the
butter into ½-inch chunks and place in the bottom of the dish.
Place the dish in the oven 5–7 minutes, or just until the butter
begins to sizzle, but no longer. While the butter is melting, layer the
eggs, milk, vanilla, maple extract, 1 teaspoon cinnamon, ⅛ teaspoon
nutmeg, flour, sugar and salt into a blender. Blend until well mixed,
about 1–2 minutes. Remove the dish from the oven and fill with
the apple slices. Sprinkle with the remaining cinnamon and nutmeg,
the allspice, and pumpkin pie spice. Bake 8 minutes to slightly
soften the apples. Remove the dish from the oven and top with
the berries and pecans. Pour the batter from the blender over
the top and sprinkle with brown sugar. Bake 20 minutes (do not
open the oven door) then remove and allow to set for 5 minutes
before cutting into desired sizes. Garnish with powdered sugar,
whipped cream, fresh berries, and cinnamon or mint leaf. Grate
fresh nutmeg on top and serve with sausage.

Ye Olde
Manor House B&B

Relax, renew, and rejuvenate at Ye Olde Manor House. Guests can luxuriate in one of our four well-appointed guest rooms, surrounded by beautiful antiques and swim in our indoor heated swimming pool. The b&b sits on three acres of lush greenery and lovely gardens, just outside of Elkhorn, Wisconsin and across the road from sparkling Lauderdale Lakes.

Ye Olde Manor House is the perfect spot for a weekend getaway or a weeklong retreat. Each morning, we prepare delicious break-

fasts with the freshest ingredients and veg-etarian, vegan, and special diet meals are happily prepared upon request. We have access to a sandy beach on nearby Pleasant Lake, a boat launch on Lauderdale Lakes, and biking and hiking in the nearby Kettle Moraine State Forest. Alpine Valley, only minutes away, offers downhill skiing in the snowy winter months and a renowned music venue in the summer. There are stables nearby for horseback riding and quaint towns with interesting antique shops, friendly cafes, and wonderful markets There are also many fine res-taurants within a short drive and the Friday night fish fry is a local tradition.

INNKEEPERS:	Karen Fulbright-Anderson & John M. Anderson
ADDRESS:	N7622 US HWY 12, Elkhorn, WI 53121
TELEPHONE:	(262) 742-2450
E-MAIL:	innkeeper@yeoldemanorhouse.com
WEBSITE:	www.yeoldemanorhouse.com
ROOMS:	4 Rooms; Private & shared baths
CHILDREN:	Inquire
PETS:	Inquire

Oven Baked Apple Pancake

Makes 6 Servings

"This dish was prepared at our post-wedding brunch
by a wonderful caterer who graciously gave us the recipe."
—INNKEEPER, *Ye Olde Manor House*

½ cup unbleached flour
½ teaspoon baking powder
½ cup plus 1 tablespoon sugar, divided
Pinch of salt
4 large eggs
1 cup milk
1 teaspoon vanilla extract
⅓ cup plus 2 tablespoons unsalted butter, divided
½ teaspoon cinnamon
½ teaspoon nutmeg
2 large green apples sliced into wedges

In a large bowl, mix together the flour, baking powder, 1 tablespoon sugar, and salt. In a separate bowl, blend the eggs, milk, vanilla, and 2 tablespoons melted butter. Mix the wet ingredients into the dry mixture and let stand 30 minutes at room temperature.

Preheat oven to 425°F. Melt the remaining ⅓ cup butter in an oven-proof skillet. In a small bowl, combine ½ cup sugar with the cinnamon and nutmeg. Sprinkle ¼ of the sugar mixture in the bottom of the skillet and set the skillet in the middle of the preheated oven. When the mixture bubbles, remove the skillet and spread the apple wedges evenly in the pan. Sprinkle the remaining sugar mixture over the apples and place the skillet over medium heat on the stove until the mixture bubbles again. Pour the batter over the apples and place in the oven for 15 minutes. Reduce oven temperature to 375°F and bake an additional 10 minutes, or until a toothpick inserted in the center comes away clean. Serve immediately.

JAY LEE INN

This Victorian Federal home, located on one acre of lake-view property, was built in 1902 by William and Carolyn Krueger. The inn is situated along the original historic path of the Elkhart Lake racetrack. Throughout the years, the property has been used as

a boarding house, an inn, and even as additional guest rooms for area resorts and hotels. The home has been completely renovated to reveal its original charm, and owners Leo and Monica thought it appropriate to re-name the home "Jay Lee Inn," the name given by Jacob and Leitha Stein back when the inn was affiliated with Pine Point Resort.

Today the inn offers a total of seven spacious guest rooms. Five of the rooms are located on the second floor and offer private baths while the two rooms located on the third floor have a shared bath. A large dining room and sitting room with piano are available for guests to enjoy during their stay. Each morning a hot gourmet breakfast is served.

INNKEEPERS: Monica & Leo Lettow
ADDRESS: 444 S Lake Street, Elkhart Lake, WI 53020
TELEPHONE: (920) 876-2910
E-MAIL: mlettow@jayleeinn.com
WEBSITE: www.jayleeinn.com
ROOMS: 7 Rooms; Private & shared baths
CHILDREN: Inquire
PETS: Inquire

Swedish Flop

Makes 8-10 Servings

*"This is a family recipe that has been a super favorite
for birthdays and any other special occasion."*

—INNKEEPER, *Jay Lee Inn*

1 cup butter, divided
2 cups flour, divided
1 cup plus 2 tablespoons water
1 teaspoon vanilla
1 cup flour
3 eggs
Chopped nuts and/or shredded coconut

CONFECTIONERS' SUGAR FROSTING
¾ cup powdered sugar
1 heaping tablespoon butter
1 heaping tablespoon Crisco
½ teaspoon vanilla extract
2 tablespoons milk

Preheat oven to 350°F. Cut ½ cup of the butter into 1 cup of flour and mix to make coarse crumbs. Sprinkle 2 tablespoons water over the flour mixture and blend quickly with a fork. Roll or pat out dough into two long strips (about 10–12 inches) on an ungreased cookie sheet. Combine 1 cup water and the remaining ½ cup butter in a saucepan and bring to a boil. Add the vanilla. Remove from heat and beat in the remaining 1 cup flour, stirring by hand with a wooden spoon. Add the eggs one at a time, beating well after each addition. Spread the dough over the pastry strips and bake 55–60 minutes, or until lightly browned. (It will flop at this point.) Allow to cool slightly before drizzling with frosting. Sprinkle with your choice of nuts, coconut, or sprinkles.

For the frosting: Mix together all ingredients, adding just 1 tablespoon of milk at first. Add additional milk to make frosting of desired consistency.

HEAVEN SCENT B&B

Heaven Scent Bed & Breakfast, a former Catholic Church, is located in the village of Randolph, Wisconsin. As you enter the former sanctuary, you will stand in awe of the beautiful hand-crafted woodwork, 21-foot-high ceilings, and original stained glass windows.

Start your day with coffee, tea, or juice before getting ready for a delicious home-cooked breakfast. Enjoy your meal in the common area in front of the gas fireplace. After breakfast, enjoy our gardens

and deck, or watch the large-screen TV. Antique shopping, fishing, hiking, sightseeing, and fine dining are just a short drive away.

Whether you are visiting family and friends or enjoying a much-needed getaway, stay with us at Heaven Scent Bed & Breakfast and relax.

INNKEEPERS:	Todd & Beth Ehlenfeldt
ADDRESS:	425 Grove Street, Randolph, WI 53956
TELEPHONE:	(920) 763-2170
E-MAIL:	heavenscentbb@centurytel.net
WEBSITE:	www.heavenscentbb.com
ROOMS:	2 Rooms
CHILDREN:	Inquire
PETS:	Resident pets only

Cinnamon Apple Belgian Waffles
Makes 4 Waffles

*"Out of our entire breakfast menu, the #1 choice is the
Cinnamon Apple Belgian Waffle. When our guests stay two nights,
they still request waffles exactly as I made them the day before.
I serve the waffles with different flavored syrups and
warm homemade applesauce."*
—INNKEEPER, *Heaven Scent B&B*

1½ cups all-purpose flour
1 tablespoons baking powder
½ teaspoon salt
¼ cup sugar
4 tablespoons melted butter
2 eggs
½ teaspoon cinnamon
½ cup buttermilk
¼ cup applesauce

Preheat waffle iron. In a mixing bowl, combine all ingredients
and whisk together until the mixture is smooth and contains no
lumps. Ladle about ⅓ cup of the mixture onto the heated waffle
iron and cook until the waffle is golden brown, about 3–4 minutes.
Repeat until all of the batter has been used.

To serve: Top the waffles with your favorite breakfast fruit, cream,
or syrup.

Egg & Breakfast Entrées

Egg & Breakfast Entrées

When in the Dairy State
do as Wisconsinites do
and enjoy the goodness of
farm-fresh eggs and gooey cheeses.

WHITE ROSE INNS

This resort oasis in the heart of Wisconsin Dells has three gorgeous bed and breakfast lodgings, plus a Gatehouse, and a Carriage House. The inns are ideal for romantic getaways or family vacations, but also for weddings and group events such as reunions and business meetings. We host murder mystery parties as well.

There are several breakfast choices including omelets, quiches, and daily specials. Each b&b guestroom includes relaxing, romantic amenities such as whirlpools, fireplaces, two-person spa showers, private balconies, and wonderful river views. Indulgences such as on-site massages, champagne, wine, and snack or spa baskets add to the aura of romance. An outdoor heated pool and beautiful gardens invite guests to stay a while and rest.

INNKEEPERS:	Mariah & Roger Boss
ADDRESS:	910 River Road, Wisconsin Dells, WI 53965
TELEPHONE:	(608) 254-4724; (800) 482-4724
E-MAIL:	info@thewhiterose.com
WEBSITE:	www.thewhiterose.com
ROOMS:	21 Rooms
CHILDREN:	Welcome
PETS:	Pet-free environment

Tortilla Espanola with Romesco Sauce

Makes 4 Servings

"This rendition of the traditional Spanish tapas dish is a thick omelet made with potatoes, eggs, and onions. It may be prepared up to three days in advance and kept refrigerated. To heat, place in a microwave or moderate oven and heat until just lightly warmed through."

—INNKEEPER, *White Rose Inns*

1 large onion, thinly sliced	3 teaspoons salt
3½ pounds Idaho potatoes	12 large eggs
(5 potatoes), peeled	4 veggie or sausage links,
½ cup olive oil	sliced thin

Preheat oven to 400°F. Cut the potatoes in half lengthwise. Place cut-side-down and thinly slice into half-moons (⅛-inch thick or less) and place in a medium roasting pan. Add the onion, ¼ cup of the oil, and half the salt and toss with hands. Cover the pan with foil and bake approximately 45 minutes. Remove the foil. In a medium bowl, beat the eggs with a wire whisk. Add the potato mixture and the remaining salt and mix. Pour the potatoes, egg mixture, and sausage into a 9x13-inch greased baking pan. Bake 45 minutes, or until firm. Serve warm or at room remperature with Romesco Sauce.

Romesco Sauce

Makes 2 Cups

"In Spain, this sauce accompanies almost everything. It keeps well in the fridge for 5 days and freezes perfectly."

—INNKEEPER, *White Rose Inns*

3 roasted red bell peppers or	1½ tablespoons chipotle peppers
1 (12 ounce) can pimientos, drained	in adobo sauce
2½ ounces slivered toasted almonds	⅓ cup olive oil
4 ounces favorite marinara sauce	1½ tablespoons balsamic vinegar
2 teaspoons minced garlic	1½ teaspoons salt

Combine all ingredients in a blender and purée until smooth.

APPLE GROVE INN

This quiet and historic country bed and breakfast, located just minutes from Bayfield and the Apostle Islands National Lakeshore, was once a 75-acre dairy and strawberry farm, owned by renowned rural Wisconsin artist, John Black. Each of the four guest

rooms has a private bath, electric fireplace, and robes for guest use.

Each morning, enjoy fruits, berries, and vegetables grown organically in our own gardens as part of your breakfast.

INNKEEPERS:	Kathy & Greg Bergner
ADDRESS:	85095 State Highway 13, Bayfield, WI 54814
TELEPHONE:	(715) 779-9558; (888) 777-9558
E-MAIL:	Kathy@applegroveinn.net
WEBSITE:	www.applegroveinn.net
ROOMS:	4 Rooms
CHILDREN:	Facility inappropriate for children
PETS:	Resident pets only

Sophia Loren Omelet

Makes 6-8 Servings

"This is one of the most popular dishes I serve at the Apple Grove Inn.
When tomatoes are in season, they add a wonderful taste of sunshine.
Bacon is also a great substitution for the ham.
For a gluten-free alternative, you can substitute rice pasta.
I adapted this recipe from an article I read about Sophia Loren."

—INNKEEPER, *Apple Grove Inn*

6 ounces whole wheat spaghetti
½ stick unsalted butter, divided
8 large eggs
3 tablespoons olive oil
1 tablespoon milk
Salt and pepper, to taste
½ cup diced ham
½ cup shredded mozzarella cheese
¼ cup finely grated Parmesan cheese
Sun-dried tomatoes, chopped

Cook the spaghetti in salted boiling water until al dente. Drain and immediately toss with 2 tablespoons butter. Whisk together the eggs, oil, milk, salt, pepper, ham, and mozzarella. Preheat broiler. Heat 2 tablespoons butter in a 12-inch non-stick, oven-proof skillet. Add the egg mixture, lifting with a heatproof spatula so the raw egg flows to the bottom of the pan. Cook until almost set, 3–5 minutes. Arrange the spaghetti over the eggs and lightly press into the egg mixture. Sprinkle with Parmesan cheese. Broil the omelet 4–6 inches from heat until the top is golden brown, 2–3 minutes. Garnish with sun-dried tomatoes and cut into wedges.

SWEET AUTUMN INN

Sweet Autumn Inn offers three guest rooms, each with a fireplace, private bathroom, guest robes, slippers, guest refrigerator, and microwave.

No boring breakfasts here! In the morning you will enjoy a full and memorable meal. Teri easily accommodates special diets: No  wheat, no eggs, no dairy, no problem! She also loves to use seasonal fruits and vegetables in her menu and grows many of them herself. From the asparagus and rhubarb in the spring to the pumpkin and apples in winter, the spicy aroma of cinnamon, cloves, nutmeg, and cardamom fill the air. Home-baked breads and fresh eggs come together to make breakfast a feast. Are your taste buds tempted yet?

"The Sweet Autumn Inn offers the
'best beds' and 'best breakfasts!' —GUEST

"Teri's personalized service and attention to
detail makes your stay extra special." —GUEST

INNKEEPER:	Teri Nelson
ADDRESS:	1019 S Main Street, Lake Mills, WI 53551
TELEPHONE:	(920) 648-8244; (888) 648-8244
E-MAIL:	innkeeper@sweetautumninn.com
WEBSITE:	www.sweetautumninn.com
ROOMS:	3 Rooms
CHILDREN:	Inquire
PETS:	Pet-free environment

Sweet Autumn Inn's Northwoods Omelet

Makes 1 Serving

"I grew up in an area of Minnesota where the use of wild rice, which my mother purchased from the local Native Americans, was common. My mother used wild rice in a number of dishes so it was just second nature to me to add this wonderful food to my morning menu."

—INNKEEPER, *Sweet Autumn Inn*

2 eggs
Parsley
¼ cup shredded
  Monterey Jack cheese
¼ cup shredded Swiss cheese
Chives
Sour cream
Paprika
Sweet Red & Ancho Chili Pepper
  Relish (Harry & David's), for garnish

NORTHWOODS FILLING
1 rib celery, diced
3-4 chopped green onions,
  or ¼ cup chopped yellow onion
1½–2 cups cooked wild rice
1 cup sautéed sliced
  Portobello mushrooms, (optional)
12 ounces bulk breakfast sausage
⅓ cup Craisins, (optional)

Beat the eggs with a fork and add in a pinch of parsley. Pour the eggs into a piping hot omelet pan sprayed with non-stick cooking spray. Cook the omelet and top with the cheeses. Spread ½ cup Northwoods filling on half of the omelet. Fold the omelet over the filling and slip from the pan onto a warm plate. Sprinkle with paprika, garnish with sour cream and relish, and sprinkle with chives and parsley. Serve warm with toast and jam.

For the Northwoods filling: Cook the rice according to package directions. Sauté the celery and onion until soft. Remove from pan and keep warm. Sauté the mushrooms in a bit of butter and olive oil. Remove from pan and mix with the celery and onion. In a large sauté pan, brown the sausage until no longer pink. Drain well. Stir in the wild rice and the celery mixture; set aside but keep warm. If using the Craisins, soften 5 minutes in enough hot water to cover. Drain, chop, and add to the wild rice mixture. You will have enough filling for several omelets.

PINE GROVE PARK B&B
GUEST HOUSE

Pine Grove Park B&B is a Wisconsin Dells bed and breakfast tucked in the middle of 55 beautiful acres near Reedsburg, Wisconsin. We are located in the southwestern part of the state and are central to many beautiful state parks and other area attractions.

Each guesthouse has a private entrance, covered porch, and large window overlooking our varying landscapes and pond. The relaxing extra-large whirlpool tub, romantic gas-stove fireplace, scrumptious country gourmet breakfast, and warm hospitality will make you wish you had discovered our prime bed and breakfast accommoda-

tions sooner!

Our charming Wisconsin Dells lodging is surrounded with lush greenery and set among sandstone outcroppings on a diverse landscape including woodlands, wetlands, oak savannahs, and native wildflower gardens. Enjoy our picturesque landscape and wildlife with a relaxing walk on our trails or just sit and reflect on a bench by the pond.

INNKEEPERS:	Jean & Kurt Johansen
ADDRESS:	S2720 County Road V, Reedsburg, WI 53959
TELEPHONE:	(608) 524-0071; (866) 524-0071
E-MAIL:	info@pinegroveparkbb.com
WEBSITE:	www.pinegroveparkbb.com
ROOMS:	4 Guest Houses
CHILDREN:	Facility inappropriate for children
PETS:	Resident pets only

Peasant Hashbrown Pie

Makes 8 Servings

*"The following recipe is my best guess for quantities,
especially of the seasonings. I don't measure when I make this,
but rather test for taste as I go."*

—INNKEEPER, *Pine Grove Park B&B Guest House*

¾ pound sweet Italian sausage, casings removed
¾ pound hot Italian sausage, casings removed
3 tablespoons butter
24 ounces Southern Style Hashbrowns,
    or 8-12 Russet potatoes, peeled and cubed
2 cups crème fraîche
Large pinch saffron (approximately ¼ teaspoon)
2 teaspoons Lawry's seasoned salt
½ teaspoon cayenne pepper, or to taste
½ teaspoon Spanish paprika
¼ teaspoon cinnamon
8 large eggs
3 cups whole milk, or mixture milk and half & half
Salt and pepper to taste
2 cups grated Cheddar cheese,
    extra sharp recommended

Preheat oven to 350°F. In a large skillet over medium-high heat, brown the Italian sausage in approximately 1 tablespoon of olive oil. Remove from the pan to drain. Add 3 tablespoons butter to the pan and cook the potatoes. In a small bowl, combine the crème fraîche and saffron. Let stand 10 minutes and stir again. When the potatoes are tender, add the seasoned salt, cayenne, paprika, and cinnamon. Add the crème fraîche and stir to combine. Add the cooked sausage to the pan and stir to blend. Divide the mixture evenly between 8 small buttered skillets, large ramekins, or gratin dishes. Press the mixture in to fit. In a large bowl, whisk together the eggs, milk, salt, and pepper. Pour evenly over the potato/sausage mixture to fill the pans. Top with the Cheddar cheese and bake approximately 30 minutes.

LAKE RIPLEY LODGE B&B

Experience the tranquility of a glistening lake with towering pine trees and escape into the romance of a sunset at the historic and charming Inn at Lake Ripley Lodge Bed and Breakfast. Located in Cambridge, Wisconsin, just ten miles southeast of Madison and fifty miles from Milwaukee, the inn is conveniently located near bike/hike/ski trails, golf, and shops. Drift into a bygone era on our grand porch swing and enjoy lakefront luxuries, whirlpools,

fireplaces, boats, and a lingering lakefront breakfast.

Lake Ripley Lodge B & B has been highlighted in the *Wisconsin State Journal, Treasures of Wisconsin,* and *Discover* magazine. We will do our best to make your stay a memorable one at this unique inn complete with scrumptious breakfasts!

INNKEEPERS:	Janice & Jim Hoiby
ADDRESS:	N4376 Friedel Avenue, Cambridge, WI 53523
TELEPHONE:	(877) 210-6195
E-MAIL:	information@lakeripley.com
WEBSITE:	www.lakeripley.com
ROOMS:	6 Rooms
CHILDREN:	Inquire
PETS:	Pet-free environment

Caramelized Onion Spinach Quiche

Makes 1 Quiche

1 pie pastry shell
1 medium white onion
3–4 Roma tomatoes
5 eggs
1 cup heavy cream
1 tablespoon ground fresh rosemary
1 teaspoon salt
1 teaspoon pepper
2 cups fresh spinach leaves

Preheat oven to 250°F and lightly bake the pastry shell. Slice the onion in half and then julienne (thinly slice). Sauté in a medium skillet or saucepan over low heat, or in the 250°F oven until brown. Thinly slice the tomato and set aside. In a medium bowl, combine the eggs, heavy cream, and spices and mix well. Remove the pie shell from the oven and increase oven temperature to 350°F.

Place the caramelized onion in the bottom of the pie shell. Place the spinach over the top of the onion. Pour the egg mixture over the onion and spinach and top with tomato slices. Bake 30–35 minutes, or until golden brown.

TUFTS' MANSION

Tufts' Mansion, located in Neillsville, Wisconsin, is a bed and breakfast like none you've ever experienced. Read a book in the parlour, sit on the front porch and relax, or stroll the beautiful grounds. You can even enjoy a soak in your own private claw-foot jetted tub.

A gourmet breakfast is served each morning in the formal dining area. On special Fridays and Saturdays you can enjoy some of the finest live music Central Wisconsin has to offer before you retire to your suite for the evening. Owners James & Dawn Voss and James

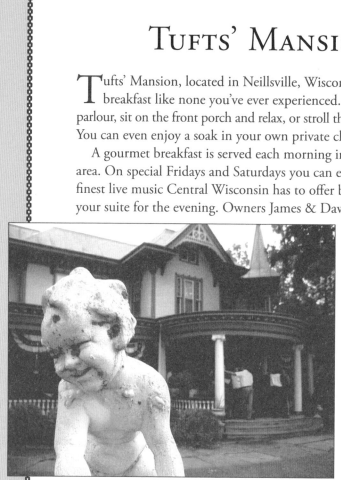

& Ellen Rickard are sure that an evening at Tufts' Mansion is a night you'll fondly remember.

Tufts' is also available for weddings, anniversaries, class reunions, and whatever special occasion you have in mind.

INNKEEPERS:	James & Dawn Voss
ADDRESS:	26 Hewett Street, Neillsville, WI 54456
TELEPHONE:	(715) 743-3346
E-MAIL:	tuftsmansion@tds.net
WEBSITE:	www.tuftsmansion.com
ROOMS:	4 Rooms
CHILDREN:	Welcome
PETS:	Welcome

Crab & Onion Quiche

Makes 1 Quiche

"This is one of our favorite recipes.
The original was found on the back of a bag of cheese,"
—INNKEEPER, *Tufts' Mansion*

8 ounces shredded imitation crab meat
3 sliced green onions
4 eggs
1¼ cups milk
¼ cup melted butter
½ cup Bisquick
½ cup shredded mozzarella
⅛ teaspoon pepper

Preheat oven to 350°F. Place the crab meat and onions together in a large greased pie pan. In a medium bowl, beat together the eggs, milk, and butter. Add the Bisquick and mix to combine. Pour the mixture over the crab and onion mixture and sprinkle with cheese. Bake 30–40 minutes.

Tips and Variations

You could use real lump crab meat in place of imitation in this recipe, but the cook time may need to be adjusted — imitation crab meat is already cooked — and the texture of the dish will be different.

CANYON ROAD INN

Canyon Road Inn is a secluded, wooded, lakeside getaway with small resort features in a spacious contemporary home. There is something for most everyone here. Enjoy the shady lakeside trails, gazebo, and benches overlooking the lake, while keeping your eyes open for songbirds and wildlife. Complimentary canoes or paddleboats provide summer fun and snowshoes are offered in the winter. The fishing is often good, so bring your rod and reel, or just enjoy the scenery. And you can always sit on a patio on "sunset point" to simply enjoy some quiet comfort with that special someone! Dry firewood is available for your evening campfire.

Breakfast is our favorite meal and many repeat guests say that it's their favorite part of a stay at Canyon Road Inn! Guests are served "Wisconsin Family Style" in the sunny dining room. In addition to our entrées, we offer muffins, bread or rolls, and a fresh or baked fruit dish along with coffee, a variety of teas, cocoa, and juices. The inn also has a guest snack area with refrigerator, microwave, and ice-

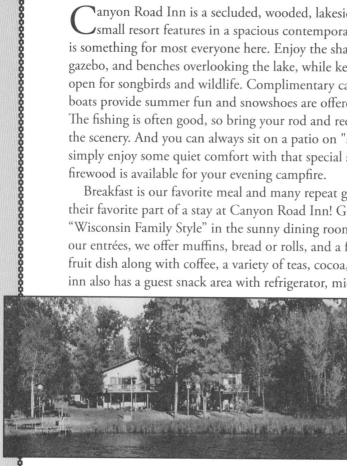

maker, stocked with glasses, ice buckets, cups, coffee, herbal teas, and cocoa.

INNKEEPERS:	Judy & Ken Ahlberg
ADDRESS:	575 W Town Line Road, Turtle Lake, WI 54889
TELEPHONE:	(715) 986-2121; (888) 251-5542
E-MAIL:	info@canyonroadinn.com
WEBSITE:	www.canyonroadinn.com
ROOMS:	5 Rooms
CHILDREN:	Inquire
PETS:	Inquire

Quiche Italiano

Makes 1 Quiche

"This light and fluffy quiche is very popular with guests and is both low-fat and gluten free. It can be easily doubled in a 9x13-inch pan for a large family. The youngsters love it as well."

—INNKEEPER, *Canyon Road Inn*

½ cup spaghetti sauce
½ cup low-fat cottage cheese
½ cup low-fat sour cream
6 large eggs
2 cups shredded mozzarella cheese
2 tablespoons grated Parmesan cheese

Preheat oven to 350°F and coat the bottom of the quiche pan with olive oil. Spread the spaghetti sauce in the bottom of the pan and top with mozzarella cheese. In a medium bowl, beat together the eggs, cottage cheese, and sour cream. Pour the egg mixture over the mozzarella and top with Parmesan. Bake 45 minutes before cutting and garnishing with small tomatoes.

Tips and Variations

To make the Mexican variation, substitute salsa for the spaghetti sauce, Monterey Jack cheese in place of the mozzarella, and Cheddar for the Parmesan. Serve with salsa on the side.

Reynolds House B&B

Reynolds House, a local landmark near downtown Sturgeon Bay, is a stately Queen Anne Victorian that has been beautifully restored to its circa 1900 grandeur. The home still features the original woodwork and leaded windows.

I serve my guests a two-course gourmet breakfast, voted "Best Breakfast" by *Arrington's Bed & Breakfast Journal's Inn Traveler*. This mouthwatering meal is served in our bright, plant-filled, circular solarium or the oak-paneled dining room. I am often asked to adapt my recipes to special diets. A recent guest dined gluten-free for almost a week, and she had the same breakfast as everyone else, even

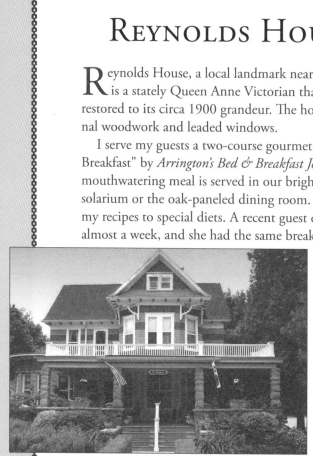

the blueberry streusel French toast! I love what I do, and it shows.

"The breakfast here is absolutely fabulous... you can run all day to see the sights and shops in the area."
—*Guest*

INNKEEPER:	Heather Hull
ADDRESS:	111 S 7th Avenue, Sturgeon Bay, WI 54235
TELEPHONE:	(920) 746-9771; (877) 269-7401
E-MAIL:	hahull@reynoldshousebandb.com
WEBSITE:	www.reynoldshousebandb.com
ROOMS:	4 Rooms
CHILDREN:	Facility inappropriate for children
PETS:	Pet-free environment

Door County Cherry Ham Strata

Plan ahead, this dish needs to be refrigerated overnight!

Makes 6 Servings

*"Reynolds House was built by William Reynolds,
whose family gained their wealth and prominence by growing
and canning Door County cherries."*
—INNKEEPER, *Reynolds House B&B*

1 loaf French bread, sliced ¼–½-inch thick
1 cup dried Door County cherries
1½ cup finely diced ham
8 ounces Swiss cheese, finely shredded
½ cup cherry syrup
10 large eggs
2¼ cups milk
1 teaspoon vanilla or cherry extract

Remove the crusts from the bread slices and grease 6 small soufflé dishes. Cover the bottom of each dish with bread. Layer cherries, ham, and cheese over the bread. Cube the remaining bread slices and sprinkle over the top of each dish. In a large bowl, combine the cherry syrup, eggs, milk, and vanilla; mix well. Divide the egg mixture evenly between the soufflé dishes. Arrange the filled dishes on a baking sheet, cover, and refrigerate overnight.

The following morning: Preheat oven to 350°F. Uncover the baking sheet and place in the oven. Bake 55–60 minutes, or until a knife inserted in the center comes away clean. Transfer the soufflés to individual plates and serve immediately. Enjoy!

Pinehaven B&B

At Pinehaven Bed and Breakfast you will find a serene, scenic setting. The tree-lined drive leads you to a view of our small spring-fed lake that flows into the Baraboo River, with the Baraboo Bluffs in the background.

We have the best of both worlds: A quiet country vacation spot within fifteen miles of all the great tourist attractions for Baraboo and Wisconsin Dells. Our guests can use the rowboat, fish (catch and release), relax in the gazebo, and enjoy the flower gardens. Many of our guests ask Lyle for a tour to see the horses as well.

INNKEEPERS:	Lyle & Marge Getschman
ADDRESS:	E13083 State Highway 33, Baraboo, WI 53913
TELEPHONE:	(608) 356-3489
E-MAIL:	pinehavenbnb@centurytel.net
WEBSITE:	www.pinehavenbnb.com
ROOMS:	4 Rooms; 1 Cottage
CHILDREN:	Inquire
PETS:	Pet-free environment

Chicken Cordon Bleu Strata

Makes 8-10 Servings

*"Chicken for breakfast? Why not! Our guests love it.
One of our regular guests proclaimed it a 'keeper' for our collection
of breakfast entrées."*

—INNKEEPER, *Pinehaven B&B*

6 cups toasted bread, cubed
¾ cup chicken broth
½ cup finely chopped celery
½ cup chopped broccoli
¼ cup chopped onion
¼ cup diced green bell pepper
¼ cup chopped carrots
2 cups diced cooked chicken
¾ cup cubed ham
¾ cup grated Swiss cheese
¾ cup mayonnaise
1 teaspoon salt
¼ teaspoon pepper
4 eggs
1½ cups milk
1 cup cubed Cheddar cheese

Preheat oven to 325°F and grease a 13x9-inch baking dish. Place the bread cubes in the bottom of the dish and pour the chicken broth evenly over the top. Gently sauté or steam the celery, broccoli, onion, bell pepper, and carrots until crisp-tender. In a medium bowl combine the chicken, ham, Swiss cheese, and vegetables. Add the mayonnaise and season with salt and pepper. Mix well and spread over the bread cubes. In a medium bowl, slightly beat the eggs. Mix in the milk and pour over the mixture. Bake 50 minutes and remove from oven and sprinkle with Cheddar cheese cubes. Return to oven for 10 minutes. Remove when the cheese is hot and bubbly and let stand 10 minutes before slicing.

DREAMS
OF YESTERYEAR B&B

Dreams of Yesteryear Bed and Breakfast is an antique embellished, National Historic Register Queen Anne Victorian. It's also the only b&b within the designated Historic Downtown Main Street Business District of Stevens Point. The inn is conveniently located in a quiet residential neighborhood amid other architectural beauties and has been featured in *Victorian Homes* magazine. Dreams is situated just one block from the Green Circle trails and

the Wisconsin River, and is conveniently located near the university, Sentry Insurance Golf Course, restaurants, and shops.

Experience historic ambiance with today's comforts while you experience the history and stories that make the Victorian era come alive. Owners Bonnie and Bill are both from Stevens Point and they invite you to share in their Victorian dream. As a guest once said, "Dreams of Yesteryear is truly the kind of place Victorian dreams are made of."

INNKEEPERS:	**Bonnie & Bill Maher**
ADDRESS:	**1100 Brawley Street, Stevens Point, WI 54481**
TELEPHONE:	**(715) 341-4525**
E-MAIL:	**bonnie@dreamsofyesteryear.com**
WEBSITE:	**www.dreamsofyesteryear.com**
ROOMS:	**6 Rooms; Private & shared baths**
CHILDREN:	**Inquire**
PETS:	**Pet-free environment**

Dreams Sausage Strata

Plan ahead, this dish needs to be refrigerated overnight!

Makes 8 Servings

*"A photo of this delightful dish is featured on my website.
Guests tell me that it tastes as good as it looks."*
—INNKEEPER, *Dreams of Yesteryear B&B*

12 slices white bread, crusts removed
¾ cup grated sharp Cheddar cheese
1 pound Italian sausage, browned
8 large eggs
3 cups milk
½ teaspoon salt
1 teaspoon garlic powder
1 teaspoon dry mustard

Grease or spray a 9x12-inch cake pan. Line the bottom of the dish with bread. Sprinkle the cheese then the sausage over the top. In a large bowl, combine the milk, eggs, and spices. Pour the mixture over the bread, cover with plastic wrap, and refrigerate overnight.

The following morning: Preheat oven to 350°F and bake 45 minutes.

St. Croix River Inn

Nestled on a bluff overlooking the St. Croix River sits the St. Croix River Inn of historic Osceola, Wisconsin. Built in 1908, this turn-of-the-century home was constructed of limestone quarried along the nearby riverbanks. Today, accommodations are luxuriously decorated with a relaxed elegance.

The St. Croix River Inn offers all of the comforts you would expect from a fine country inn. Every room is equipped with a queen-sized bed, fireplace, hydrotherapy bath, mini-fridge, and Radio/CD player discreetly situated so as not to be a disruption. Enjoy the luxury bath products and elegant bathrobes, delight in the well-stocked entertainment cabinet offering a selection of CDs, DVDs, games, and books for use during your stay, or take time out for a health-building workout in the fitness room. Awaken refreshed and savor the flavors of a gourmet breakfast served privately in your room. Complimentary coffee, tea, and snacks are available in the lobby.

INNKEEPERS:	Ben & Jennifer Bruno & Cheryl Conarty
ADDRESS:	305 River Street, Osceola, WI 54020
TELEPHONE:	(715) 294-4248; (800) 645-8820
E-MAIL:	innkeeper@stcroixriverinn.com
WEBSITE:	www.stcroixriverinn.com
ROOMS:	7 Rooms
CHILDREN:	Facility inappropriate for children
PETS:	Pet-free environment

Fiesta Frittata

Makes 8-12 Servings

*"This dish was inspired by the Atkins craze.
It's a great start to the day and is high in protein
and good carbs. It's also a perfect reflection of
Ms. Conarty's true Southern hospitality."*
—INNKEEPER, *St. Croix River Inn*

8 ounces Cheddar Jack cheese, shredded
1 (15 ounce) can black beans
1 (15.25 ounce) can whole kernel corn
1 (10 ounce) can RoTel tomatoes
   and green chiles
Garlic and herb seasoning
10 eggs
1½ cups milk
2 teaspoons baking powder
½–1 cup sour cream

Preheat oven to 350°F and spray two pie dishes with non-stick cooking spray. Cover the bottom of each dish with cheese. Drain the beans, corn, and tomatoes well and then mix together. Divide the mixture evenly between the two pie plates and sprinkle with seasoning. In a large bowl, blend together the eggs, milk, baking powder, and sour cream and pour into the pie dishes. Bake 45 minutes, or until a knife inserted in the center comes away clean. Cut and serve.

Tips and Variations

Sprinkle with shredded cheese, sliced green onions, and a splash of salsa. Garnish with seasoned tomatoes and sliced avocado.

Homemade black beans, fresh corn, tomatoes, and chiles are preferable when available.

Crystal River Inn B&B, llc

Our Crystal River Inn B&B is the heart of the 1853 Andrew Potts farmstead. In keeping with this heritage, breakfast is a full, hot, delicious meal prepared with down-home flavor and features our homemade bread and our own jellies made from native fruit such as wild grapes, plums, and high bush cranberry. Robert sometimes adds Southern flair from his native Louisiana: biscuits, sausage gravy, cornbread... We delight in fixing meals for special diets such as gluten-free and vegetarian.

In our effort to be "green," we use local produce and fruit and vegetables from our garden when available. We serve pure Wisconsin maple syrup and brew only fair trade, organic coffee.

INNKEEPERS:	Deb & Robert Benada
ADDRESS:	E1369 Rural Road, Waupaca, WI 54981
TELEPHONE:	(715) 258-5333; (800) 236-5789
E-MAIL:	crystalriverinn@charterinternet.com
WEBSITE:	www.crystalriver-inn.com
ROOMS:	7 Rooms; 2 Cottages
CHILDREN:	Inquire
PETS:	Resident pets only

Helen's Breakfast Soufflé

Plan ahead, this dish needs to be refrigerated overnight!

Makes 8 Servings

Adapted from Helen Potts Robinson in the
Parfreyville UMC Anniversary Cookbook *by Robert Benada.*

8 slices white or wheat bread,
   torn or cubed
2 tablespoons dried onion
2 cups Cheddar cheese, grated
8 eggs
4 cups milk
1 teaspoon salt*
¼ teaspoon pepper
2 dashes Tabasco sauce, to taste
Chives

Place the bread cubes in a greased 9x13-inch baking dish and sprinkle the dried onion over the top. Spread the cheese over the bread cubes. In a medium bowl, beat together the eggs, milk, salt, pepper, and Tabasco sauce. Pour the egg mixture over the bread and cheese layer, sprinkle on chives, cover, and refrigerate overnight.

The following morning: Preheat oven to 350°F and bake 1 hour. To prepare individual servings, place ⅛ of the mixture into a greased shallow oven-proof dish and bake 35–40 minutes.

Tips and Variations

In place of salt, use ¼ teaspoon of Penzey's Fox Point Seasoning per egg. Green Jalapeno Tabasco is also great on this dish and is far less hot than standard Tabasco. Try adding ½–1 cup chopped turkey, ham, or for a meatless version, add 2 portobello veggie burgers.

LINDSAY HOUSE B&B

Come rest your mind, relax your body, and rejuvenate your spirit at the Lindsay House Bed & Breakfast. Our lovely 1892 Victorian home is filled with an eclectic mix of furnishings. All of our rooms have handcrafted queen-size beds and private bathrooms. Each morning we offer a delicious variety of full breakfast options. After, enjoy one of our many outdoor seating areas including the wrap-around porch and our beautiful gardens.

We are located in lovely Manawa, in the Central Wisconsin River Region at the center of Waupaca County. There are many year-round outdoor activities surrounding us including the Mid-Western Rodeo, the Iola Car Show, the Waupaca Strawberry Festival, and Manawa's own Santaland.

INNKEEPERS:	Judy & Tim Trull
ADDRESS:	539 Depot Street, Manawa, WI 54949
TELEPHONE:	(920) 596-3643; (877) 778-8758
E-MAIL:	lhousebb@wolfnet.net
WEBSITE:	www.lindsayhouse.com
ROOMS:	4 Rooms
CHILDREN:	Inquire
PETS:	Inquire

Sunshine Eggs Benedict

Makes 2 Servings

2 split English muffins
1 teaspoon butter
Splash of white vinegar
4 eggs, poached
1 avocado
1 Roma tomato
1 bunch garlic chives, diced

HOLLANDAISE SAUCE
3 egg yolks
1 tablespoon lemon juice, fresh or bottled
Dash of white pepper
1 stick butter, melted

Spread the butter on the English muffin halves and place on a grill pan and toast. Wrap in foil and keep them warm in the oven until ready to serve. Fill a frying pan with approximately 3 inches of water and the vinegar and bring to a strong simmer. Crack the eggs into a small ramekin, one at a time, and slide into the hot water. Poach them until the whites are set and place on a plate. Cover and keep warm in the oven. Slice the avocado and tomato and set aside.

To make the hollandaise: Place the egg yolks, lemon juice, and pepper together in a blender. When you are ready to plate the benedict, melt the butter in a microwave and pour into the running blender, blend an additional 30 seconds after adding. Place two muffin halves on each plate and top each with a slice of tomato and a slice of avocado. Top with a poached egg and pour the hollandaise over. Sprinkle with chopped chives and serve with breakfast meat.

SILL'S LAKESHORE B&B RESORT

Come see the best the Northwoods has to offer! Sill's is an elegant lakefront property tucked away in a tranquil setting and featuring two separate guest houses/cottages as well as a whole separate floor in the main house containing a two-room suite, all set up with privacy in mind.

We've combined resort flair and a traditional bed and breakfast stay for the ultimate Northwoods experience. The resort is located just steps from downtown Minocqua and its shopping, antiquing, and great dining. Bike or hike the Bearskin Trail right outside your door, or jump into a canoe, kayak, or paddleboat right on the prop-

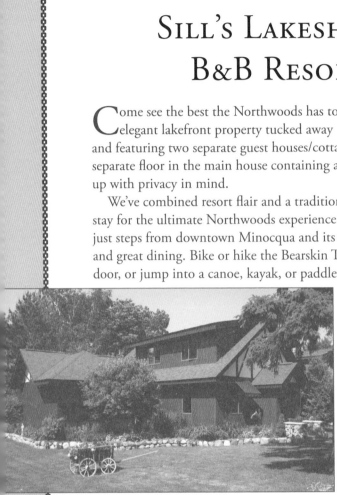

erty. Rent a pontoon for a long, lazy afternoon on our chain of lakes, or just sit out on the piers (with fishing pole or not), docks, or decks and enjoy the beautiful view while enjoying a glass of wine.

INNKEEPERS:	Ron & Lori Sill
ADDRESS:	130 Lakeshore Drive, Minocqua, WI 54548
TELEPHONE:	(715) 356-3384
E-MAIL:	sills@newnorth.net
WEBSITE:	www.sillslakeshorebandb.com
ROOMS:	3 Rooms
CHILDREN:	Inquire
PETS:	Pet-free environment

Eggs Charleston

Makes 1 Serving

"The flavors come from one of Chef Ron's favorite cities."
—INNKEEPER, *Sill's Lakeshore B&B Resort*

2 tablespoons butter, divided
2 tablespoons chopped onion
2 tablespoons chopped red bell pepper
¼ teaspoon chopped fresh chives
⅛ teaspoon tarragon
2 extra large eggs
2–3 large fresh shrimp,
   butterfly and cut in half
3 stalks fresh asparagus,
   steamed and cut into 1-inch pieces
⅛ cup cold water or milk
¼ cup Swiss cheese, grated
Lemon pepper seasoning, to taste
Béarnaise sauce

Melt 1 tablespoon butter in a large skillet over medium heat. Add the onion, bell pepper, chives, and tarragon and cook 3 minutes, stirring frequently. Add the asparagus and shrimp to the skillet and cook until the shrimp turn bright pink. Remove from heat and cover. In a bowl, beat together the eggs and milk or water. Fold in the cheese and season with lemon pepper. Melt the remaining butter in a clean skillet over medium-high heat. Pour in the cooked vegetables and shrimp and pour in the egg mixture. Sauté until eggs are cooked. Plate and garnish with prepared Béarnaise sauce (Knorr's brand recommended) and additional Swiss cheese.

WILLOW POND BED, BREAKFAST & EVENTS

Located halfway between Appleton and Stevens Point, just five miles north of Weyauwega, Wisconsin, a masterpiece of nature awaits your visit. Take a walk in the spectacular gardens, relax by the pond and waterfalls, and breathe in the fresh air of the country.

The farmhouse, built in 1901, has been a showcase for Renee's antique furniture collection. Recently, Joe & Renee took on the task of restoring the home to its original design with the goal of making the farmhouse available for the public to view and to provide a place for people in the area to stay. With more people wanting to hold their special events at Willow Pond, Joe & Renee decided to provide additional services such as event planning and receptions.

There are many locations on the twelve acres at Willow Pond to hold your reception or other celebration. From tea parties out in the garden to receptions by the pond and waterfalls, they can put up a tent and you can have your event, rain or shine. If you choose to have your party indoors, the reception room in the barn is also available for your group.

INNKEEPERS:	Joe & Renee Wyngaard
ADDRESS:	E5490 North Shore Road, Weyauwega, WI 54983
TELEPHONE:	(920) 867-2493
E-MAIL:	renee@willowpondevents.com
WEBSITE:	www.willowpondevents.com
ROOMS:	5 Rooms
CHILDREN:	Welcome
PETS:	Please Inquire

Pillowtalk Eggs

Makes 12 Servings

"I came up with this recipe for the Red Hat Ladies.
They come to visit in their pajamas every year."
—INNKEEPER, *Willow Pond Bed, Breakfast & Events*

1 roll puff pastry
½ cup onion, chopped
1 cup asparagus, chopped
½ cup red bell pepper, chopped
½ cup yellow bell pepper, chopped
½ cup chopped ham or sausage
1½ tablespoons butter
Salt
Pepper
12 eggs
Hollandaise sauce
Paprika

Preheat oven to 400°F. Line the bottom of 12 muffin cups with rounds of puff pastry, reserving 12 same-sized rounds for the "pillow tops." Sauté the onion, asparagus, bell peppers, and ham or sausage in a medium skillet with butter. Season with salt and pepper, and additional seasonings of choice, to taste. Divide the vegetable/ham mixture evenly between the 12 muffin cups and top with the reserved puff pastry rounds. Bake approximately 20 minutes, until nicely browned. Poach 12 eggs.

To serve: Carefully remove from the muffin cups and place on individual plates. Top each with a poached egg and cover with Hollandaise. Sprinkle with paprika to garnish.

Brumder Mansion B&B

George Brumder, the heir to a prominent German language publishing business, built this majestic home in 1910. The architecture of the mansion is a blend of Victorian and Arts and Crafts elements. Common rooms feature fireplaces and exquisite woodwork, and the entire home is furnished with lovely antiques. The formality and elegance of the interior contrasts with the home's overall atmosphere of relaxation and warmth.

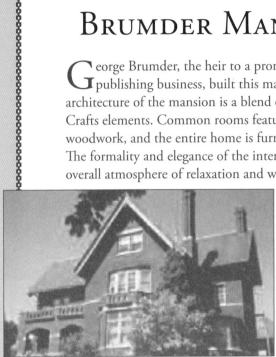

Explore and enjoy the antique books, photo albums, and china collection, warm yourself by a roaring fire, or enjoy an early morning cup of coffee out on the front porch while you peruse the paper. Request a couple's massage or sip champagne while in your opulent whirlpool. Let us help you customize your Milwaukee visit to make it as special and memorable as you'd like it to be.

ADDRESS:	3046 W Wisconsin Avenue, Milwaukee, WI 53208
TELEPHONE:	(414) 342-9767; (866) 793-3676
E-MAIL:	brumder@yahoo.com
WEBSITE:	www.brumdermansion.com
ROOMS:	6 Rooms
CHILDREN:	Children age 5 and older welcome
PETS:	Pet-free environment

Ham & Egg Crêpes

Makes 4 Servings

*"This recipe was adapted from one found
on the Mr. Breakfast website."*
—*Innkeeper, Brumder Mansion B&B*

1 batch of crêpes
¾ cup sour cream
1 cup cooked ham,
    chopped into ¼-inch cubes
6 hard boiled eggs, chopped
1 tablespoon chopped chives
¼ teaspoon dry mustard
1 (10 ounce) can cream of chicken soup
¼ cup milk
¼ cup Parmesan cheese

Preheat oven to 350°F. Lightly spray a 13x9-inch baking dish with
non-stick cooking spray. In a large bowl, mix together the sour
cream, ham, eggs, chives, and dry mustard with half of the soup;
set aside. In a separate bowl, mix the remaining soup with the
milk and half of the cheese. Fill each crêpe with ¼ cup of the ham
filling and roll. Repeat until all of the crêpes and filling have been
used and arrange in the prepared baking dish. Cover with the
sauce and sprinkle with the remaining cheese. Bake 30 minutes.

HAMILTON HOUSE B&B

This 1861 Second Empire home with spacious guest rooms and a variety of common areas offers you just the escape you need. Sun-filled parlors provide a tranquil haven for reading, parlor games, or quiet conversation. Guestrooms feature a cozy bed, whirlpool and/or fireplace. Guests are invited to use the stocked refreshment center complete with microwave and fridge. In the morning, take your time as you sip coffee in your room as you prepare for a full breakfast served in the formal dining room by firelight.

We are centrally located for a variety of activities including: horseback riding, hiking, biking, kayaking, rock climbing, theater, shopping, and spas.

INNKEEPERS:	**Jim & Kathleen Fleming**
ADDRESS:	**328 W Main Street, Whitewater, WI 53190**
TELEPHONE:	**(262) 473-1900**
E-MAIL:	**kathie@bandbhamiltonhouse.com**
WEBSITE:	**www.bandbhamiltonhouse.com**
ROOMS:	**8 Rooms**
CHILDREN:	**Inquire**
PETS:	**Pet-free environment**

Eggs to Go

Makes 12 Servings

*"My mother and I developed this for the men in our lives
who must leave early for work. We make up a batch of these
at the beginning of the week. Then everyone warms one or two
on their way out the door in the morning. These are easy
to eat during the morning commute with a cup of coffee.
Any meat and vegetable combination may be used.
My favorite is ham and spinach. Broccoli and turkey sausage
is a great option as well."*
—INNKEEPER, *Hamilton House B&B*

6 eggs, lightly beaten
3 tablespoons butter, melted
1½ cups chopped deli ham
½ cup dry unseasoned bread crumbs
¼ cup shredded Cheddar cheese
1 tablespoon minced chives

Preheat oven to 375°F and grease 12 muffin cups. Mix the ingredients together in a medium bowl and divide evenly between the greased cups. Bake 15–20 minutes and serve warm or store in the refrigerator and heat in the microwave as needed.

Gresley House B&B

The Gresley House B&B is located on 20 acres of farmstead land in Milwaukee's North Shore area. The house, which dates back to 1861, was a community center of sorts, hosting activities after

weddings and funerals, and at the conclusion of harvest seasons.

Today we offer the house and grounds as a peaceful place to get away and relax, as a lodging alternative for the business traveler interested in a less institutional setting, or simply as a home base while visiting family and friends or attractions in the area. We offer comfortable accommodations and surroundings (we are not a museum) with a full breakfast each morning, including beverages, granola and yogurt, a variety of fruit and muffins, and an egg dish or maybe even waffles.

INNKEEPERS:	John & Ruth Gresley
ADDRESS:	13907 N Port Washington Road, Mequon, WI 53097
TELEPHONE:	(262) 387-9980; (888) 270-3875
E-MAIL:	innkeepers@gresleyhouse.com
WEBSITE:	www.gresleyhouse.com
ROOMS:	4 Rooms; Private & shared baths
CHILDREN:	Inquire
PETS:	Inquire

Baked Eggs

Makes 1 Serving

*"This recipe serves one person and will probably be adequate
for most people when served with other breakfast items.
You can easily increase or decrease the number of eggs
and the size of the baking dish to suit your guests' appetites.
You may want to slightly adjust the other ingredients as well.
I always take a moment to explain the ingredients to our guests,
most enjoy knowing how the dish was prepared."*

—INNKEEPER, *Gresley House B&B*

½ tablespoon butter
¼ cup grated Parmesan cheese
2 eggs
Dash of nutmeg
2–3 tomato slices, recommend Roma
¼ teaspoon basil
1–2 links sausage

Preheat oven to 350°F and coat the bottom of a 7-inch au gratin dish with butter. Sprinkle cheese over the bottom and sides of the dish. Crack the eggs into the dish and sprinkle with nutmeg. Bake, uncovered, 12–14 minutes (just until yolks are solid). Check the eggs occasionally for bubbles that can develop in the whites.

While the eggs cook, heat the sausage according to package directions. When the eggs are done, add the tomato slices to one end of the dish. Sprinkle basil over the eggs and tomato. Cut the sausage into chunks and add to the other end of the dish. Serve with a smile!

JESSE STONE HOUSE

The Jesse Stone House

Bed & Breakfast

Waltz in the parlor amidst the turn-of-the-century décor to the player piano's vintage Tin Pan Alley music, sip tea from antique china by the victrola, or wind up the 19th century music box and remember the time you first enjoyed such a delight. For a quiet respite, enjoy the luxury of the library and its wide selection of materials, or simply stroll the majestic grounds and admire the picture perfect gardens.

Located in southeast Wisconsin and nestled along the shores of the beautiful Rock River, The Jesse Stone House is open year round and features two unique guest rooms. Jesse's Room is a grand room furnished in the dapper style to which Mr. Stone was accustomed. With its green carnation scroll wallpaper, hand-carved headboard, and well-appointed furnishings, visitors are sure to enjoy this elegant bedroom. In Sarah's Room, the Victorian rose and floral wallpaper sets an elegant tone for this large, west side bedroom with garden view. The room features a traditional washbasin and a queen bed with a handcrafted wood headboard in the ornamental style that was in vogue at the turn of the century.

INNKEEPERS:	Charles & Pat Damaske
ADDRESS:	300 S Washington Street, Watertown, WI 53094
TELEPHONE:	(920) 262-1918
E-MAIL:	info@jessestonehouse.com
WEBSITE:	www.jessestonehouse.com
ROOMS:	2 Rooms
CHILDREN:	Inquire
PETS:	Resident pets only

Breakfast Bake

Makes 4 Servings

"This dish is easily prepared the night before.
The smell of this breakfast bake greets the guests in the morning
with the smells of spicy sausage, bacon, peppers, and onions."

—INNKEEPER, *Jesse Stone House B&B*

½ pound Jimmy Dean pork sausage,
　browned and drained
¼ pound bacon, cooked and diced
1 cup shredded frozen hash brown potatoes
½ green bell pepper, chopped
½ red bell pepper, chopped
¼ cup onions, chopped
1 cup shredded co-jack cheese, divided
½ cup Bisquick
1½ cups milk
¼ teaspoon salt
2–3 large eggs

Preheat oven to 375°F. In a large bowl, mix together the sausage, bacon, frozen hash browns, peppers, onions, and ¼ cup cheese. Separate into 4 2-cup baking dishes. In a medium bowl, combine the Bisquick, milk, salt, and eggs and divide evenly between the four dishes. Spread the remaining cheese over the top and bake 30–35 minutes. Let stand 10 minutes before plating. Top with a dollop of sour cream and a few additional pieces of peppers. We serve this dish with English muffins, homemade preserves, fresh, seasonal fruit, and our Blueberry Coffee Cake.

Tips and Variations

You can easily double this recipe. Simply bake in a 9x13-inch dish.

Appetizers, Soups, Salads, & Sides

Appetizers, Soups, Salads, & Sides

*The bounty of Wisconsin farmers'
markets produced this wonderfully
mixed bag of recipes to carry you
through all four seasons.*

BRAMBLEBERRY B&B

Enjoy a romantic weekend in the country. Relax and reconnect in our beautiful and comfortable English country-style home. Warm and inviting guest rooms feature elegant canopy beds, whirlpools, and fireplaces.

Walk our wooded trails and gardens, or pet our sheep. Visit a nearby winery, brewery, or antique shops. Bike local trails, hike or ski state parks, and canoe the Black River.

We serve a wonderful three-course, candlelit breakfast in our Scottish Highland inspired dining room. Selections include our own delicious homegrown pork, eggs, and organic produce, and many of our menus are adapted from British, Scottish, or Irish recipes. We take pride in serving delicious and unique entrées.

INNKEEPERS:	Sherry & Chris Hardie
ADDRESS:	N3684 Claire Road, Taylor, WI 54659
TELEPHONE:	(608) 525-8001
E-MAIL:	innkeeper@brambleberrybandb.com
WEBSITE:	www.brambleberrybandb.com
ROOMS:	4 Rooms
CHILDREN:	Facility inappropriate for children
PETS:	Pet-free environment

Scottish Eggs

Makes 8 Eggs

"Our Scottish egg recipe was featured in the Milwaukee Journal Sentinel *and is adapted from* Great British Cooking. *In Scotland, the pubs deep-fry these tasty morsels and use quails' eggs. We use eggs from our chickens and our home-grown sausage, and bake them."*

—INNKEEPER, *Brambleberry B&B*

8 hard-boiled eggs, peeled
2 pounds ground pork sausage
2 teaspoons mace
2 tablespoons fresh chopped chives,
    or 1 tablespoon dried
¾ teaspoon ground black pepper
2 beaten eggs plus 1 tablespoon water

CRUMB MIXTURE
1⅓ cups dried bread crumbs
1½ teaspoons sage
1 teaspoon chives

Preheat oven to 350°F. In a medium bowl, combine the pork sausage, mace, chives, and pepper; mix well. Divide the mixture into eight equal portions. Flatten and wrap the sausage around each boiled egg, completely covering it. In a small bowl, beat the two eggs with the tablespoon of water. In a separate small bowl, combine the bread crumbs, sage, and chives for the crumb mixture. Dip each sausage covered egg in the beaten egg mixture, then roll each on the bread crumb mixture. Place the eggs on a baking sheet and bake 35–40 minutes, until sausage is cooked and the bread crumb mixture begins to brown. Serve hot or cold.

MARTHA'S ETHNIC B&B

Martha's Ethnic is the best bed and breakfast value. We offer many gourmet breakfast choices, wake up coffee, fresh-baked old-world kolaches or kuchen, and afternoon wine and cheese, or tea and sweet breads.

Nearby attractions include: Amish Community, Historical Village, Mini-Golf, Dairylicious Days in June, Pioneer Rendezvous Days in September, and public hunting and fishing nearby. There are also bike trails nearby and Wisconsin Dells is just a short drive away.

INNKEEPER:	Martha Polacek
ADDRESS:	259 E 2nd Street, Westfield, WI 53964
TELEPHONE:	(608) 296-3361
E-MAIL:	marthasethincbandb@yahoo.com
WEBSITE:	www.wbba.org/inns/MarthasEthnicBB_Westfield_WI.html
ROOMS:	3 Rooms
CHILDREN:	Inquire
PETS:	Pet-free environment

Date Rounds

Plan ahead, this needs to refrigerate overnight!

Makes 4-6 Servings

*"I have used this recipe for over 45 years.
It is a simple holiday favorite. We also serve old-world lebkuchen,
shortbread, and kolatches."*
—INNKEEPER, *Martha's Ethnic B&B*

1½ cups chopped dates
1½ cups chopped nuts
1 (14 ounce) can sweetened condensed milk
Ritz crackers

GARNISH
3 ounces cream cheese
1½ cups powdered sugar
3–6 tablespoons cream

In a medium bowl, combine the dates, nuts, and condensed milk. Cover and refrigerate overnight.

The following morning: Preheat oven to 350°F. Remove the date mixture from the fridge and place a spoonful on a Ritz cracker. Place the cracker on a sheet pan and repeat until all the date mixture has been used. Bake 10 minutes. In a medium bowl, mix together the cream cheese, powdered sugar, and cream to make a frosting-like garnish. Drizzle the frosting over the topped crackers. Do not store leftovers in Tupperware. Store in a metal cake pan covered with aluminum foil.

Woodenheart Inn

Woodenheart Inn is located on the north side of Sister Bay, in beautiful Door County. As a guest in our log home you will find your surroundings to be elegant, private, and very comfortable. Each of the five guest quarters has its own unique charm. All of the rooms have a private bath and twin, king, or queen beds.

Guests enjoy early morning coffee in the guest loft or gazebo on the back deck, and there's plenty of space for late evening conversation in the great room with its large stone fireplace. A full country breakfast is served each morning in the dining room.

INNKEEPERS: **John & Judy Hurlburt**
ADDRESS: **11086 State Highway 42, Sister Bay, WI 54234**
TELEPHONE: **(920) 854-9097; (877) 854-9097**
E-MAIL: **innkeeper@woodenheart.com**
WEBSITE: **www.woodenheart.com**
ROOMS: **5 Rooms**
CHILDREN: **Inquire**
PETS: **Pet-free environment**

Raspberry Snowball

Makes 8 Servings

16 ounces cream cheese, softened

$2/_3$ cup grated Swiss cheese

½ cup chopped nuts

10 ounces frozen raspberries

1 tablespoon cornstarch

In a medium bowl, combine the cream cheese, Swiss cheese, and nuts. Shape into a ball and refrigerate. Thaw the berries; drain and reserve the liquid. In a small saucepan over medium-high heat, combine the cornstarch and the reserved juice from the berries. Cook until thickened. Cool slightly and then add the raspberries. Chill.

To serve: Pour the berry sauce over the cheese ball and serve with crackers.

Tips and Variations

The classic cheese ball is so versatile, you can almost use any savory or sweet combination of ingredients. Try mixing 2 tablespoons port wine with the cream cheese. Substitute shredded Cheddar, dried cranberries, and chopped pecans in place of the Swiss, nuts, and raspberries, and drizzle with real Wisconsin maple syrup for a sweet variation. Another great combination is prepared pesto and chopped sun-dried tomatoes. Mix with the cheese and roll in a savory almond salad topper.

Trollhaugen Lodge

Our bed and breakfast inn has the homey feel of a guesthouse. Uniquely decorated rooms with queen beds are romantic, cozy retreats for adults only. Choose a first-floor room with or without a wood-burning fireplace, a second-floor room with a balcony, or our second floor mini-suite featuring a king poster bed, a double sofa sleeper, gas fireplace, entertainment center, refrigerator, microwave, coffeemaker, wet bar, and a private deck with table and chairs.

Our guests enjoy a hot and cold breakfast buffet and afternoon treats.

Walk to the waterfront for sunsets and the center of town for shopping and dining, enjoy our nearby hiking trail, or relax in our outdoor whirlpool.

INNKEEPERS:	Norma & Terry Street
ADDRESS:	10176 HWY 42, Ephraim, WI 54211
TELEPHONE:	(920) 854-2713; (800) 854-4118
E-MAIL:	trollhaugen@dcwis.com
WEBSITE:	www.trollhaugenlodge.com
ROOMS:	5 Rooms
CHILDREN:	Facility inappropriate for children
PETS:	Pet-free environment

Giardiniera Bruschetta

Plan ahead, the giardiniera will require 3 nights in the refrigerator!

Makes 10 Servings

GIARDINIERA

2 green bell peppers, diced

2 red bell peppers, diced

8 fresh jalapenos, sliced

2 celery stalks, diced

2 medium carrots, sliced thin

1 small yellow onion, chopped

½ cup fresh cauliflower florets

1 bunch small asparagus tips

$^2/_3$ cup salt

Water to cover

2 cloves garlic, finely chopped

1 tablespoon dried oregano

1 teaspoon red pepper flakes

½ teaspoon black pepper

1 (5 ounce) jar pimento-stuffed
   green olives, chopped

1 cup white vinegar

1 cup extra-virgin olive oil

BRUSCHETTA

2 large tomatoes, chopped

2–3 cloves garlic, chopped

1 tablespoon extra-virgin olive oil

1 tablespoon red wine vinegar

5–6 basil leaves, chopped

2–4 sprigs chopped parsley

Salt and pepper, to taste

1 loaf Italian bread

For the giardiniera: Place the first eight ingredients in a bowl and stir in the salt. Fill with enough water to cover. Cover the dish and refrigerate overnight. The next day, drain and rinse the vegetables. In a bowl, combine the garlic, oregano, pepper, and olives. Pour in the vinegar and oil and mix well. Combine with the vegetable mixture, cover, and refrigerate two days before using.

For the bruschetta: Mix all ingredients except the bread and let sit 2 hours (serve at room temperature). Cut the bread into ¾-inch thick slices and brush with olive oil. Broil approximately 1 minute, until toasted. Thinly spread the bruschetta mixture over the toasted bread and top with a thin layer of giardiniera to serve.

Sunnyfield Farm B&B

If you like country, you're sure to take pleasure from Sunnyfield Farm Bed and Breakfast. One hundred and sixty acres of rich farmland and scenic bluffs surround this impeccably decorated turn-of-the-century farmhouse. Enjoy panoramic views of the bluffs and wildlife from the old-fashioned porch swing.

This three-story home provides three roomy bedrooms, all located on the second floor, and each featuring hardwood floors, country décor, and handmade quilts. The Rose Room has an adjoining room

with twin beds making it perfect for families or groups. The third floor offers a unique studio with accommodations for a romantic retreat, a writer's paradise, or a home away from home.

INNKEEPER:	Susanne Soltvedt
ADDRESS:	N6692 Batko Road, Camp Douglas, WI 54618
TELEPHONE:	(608) 427-3686; (888) 839-0232
E-MAIL:	soltvedt@mwt.net
WEBSITE:	www.sunnyfield.net
ROOMS:	4 Rooms; Private & shared baths
CHILDREN:	Welcome
PETS:	Welcome

Redneck Caviar

Plan ahead, this dish needs to be refrigerated overnight!

Makes About 6 Cups

*"This recipe is adapted from one found
in an Alabama church cookbook."*

—INNKEEPER, *Sunnyfield Farm*

1 (15 ounce) can black beans
1 (15 ounce) can black-eyed peas
1 (11 ounce) can shoepeg corn
2 (10 ounce) cans Ro-Tel
1 (14.5 ounce) can chopped tomatoes
1 teaspoon garlic salt
1 teaspoon garlic powder
1 teaspoon parsley flakes
1 teaspoon onion flakes
1 large bottle Italian dressing
Frito scoops

Open and drain the black beans, black-eyed peas, and corn and pour them together into a large bowl. Add, but do not drain, the Ro-Tel and chopped tomatoes. Stir in the garlic salt, garlic powder, parsley, and onion. Pour in the Italian dressing, cover the bowl, and refrigerate overnight. Serve with Fritos.

BELLE ISLE INN

Warmth, character and history envelop you upon entering the Belle Isle Inn. Built in 1910, and once used as a boarding-house for teachers, this house was meant to be shared. Located in charming Algoma, Wisconsin, surrounded by Lake Michigan, Door County, Green Bay, and picturesque Kewaunee County, Belle Isle

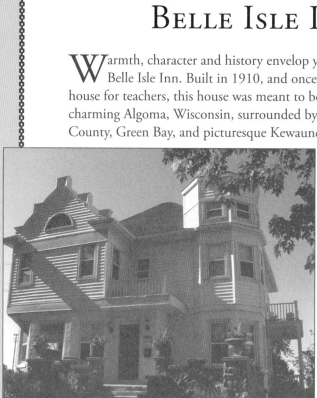

Inn is the perfect destination

The inn has a wonderful blend of yesterday's antiques and today's technology with a comfortable "home away from home" feeling. Enjoy irresistible gourmet breakfasts in the breakfast room or on the go. Evenings at the Inn include wine and appetizers by the fire or on the patio. For entertainment we have WiFi, Wii, NFL Sunday Ticket, satellite TV, movie channels, games, books and much more.

INNKEEPERS:	Tia & Scott Bellisle
ADDRESS:	617 Fremont Street, Algoma, WI 54201
TELEPHONE:	(920) 737-7733
E-MAIL:	tia@belleisleinn.com
WEBSITE:	www.belleisleinn.com
ROOMS:	4 Rooms; Shared baths
CHILDREN:	Children age 12 and older welcome
PETS:	Pet friendly

CCQ Chili Con Queso

Makes 7 Cups

6 tablespoons butter

1 medium sweet onion

3 cloves garlic, minced

8–10 hot jalapeno slices

1 teaspoon sea salt

1 teaspoon fresh ground pepper

½ teaspoon liquid habanero chili sauce

Dash of nutmeg

½ cup flour

1 quart milk

8–10 ounces each, sharp Cheddar,
    pepper Jack, and co-Jack cheese, cubed

Melt the butter in a large soup pot. Add the chopped onion, garlic, and jalapenos and sauté until soft. Grind the salt and pepper into the pot and then add the chili sauce and nutmeg. Stir in the flour to create a paste. Add the milk slowly, one cup at a time, while the roux thickens. Add the cheese a few chunks at a time and stir until melted. Place a tortilla in a bowl and pour the CCQ in to serve.

Tips and Variations

For smoother CCQ, whip the dip with a beater before serving. Try substituting other cheeses like smoked provolone or gouda, two year sharp white Cheddar, Colby, brick, or farmer's cheese. Add cayenne pepper for extra spice.

FRANKLIN STREET INN

For six years, the sign by the front door of the Franklin Street Inn has read as follows: "Enter as Strangers, Leave as Friends!" All our customer service is handled with that approach; our passion is to serve others. When guests leave, we want them to take away a memory that exceeded their expectations. We have found so many small touches to offer our guests; they call it "attention to detail." We are glad that guests appreciate what is offered here.

Running a small business, we can personally deliver our philosophy "to treat others the way we would like to be treated!" We personalize our service to accommodate every guest's needs. Our branding statement is "Franklin Street Inn... where royal treatment begins!" Let us personally invite YOU to our inn so that we may open our door of hospitality to YOU!

INNKEEPERS: Judy & Ron Halma

ADDRESS: 318 East Franklin Street, Appleton, WI 54911

TELEPHONE: (920) 993-1711; (888) 993-1711

E-MAIL: info@franklinstreetinn.com

WEBSITE: www.franklinstreetinn.com

ROOMS: 4 Rooms

CHILDREN: Children age 5 and older welcome

PETS: Pet-free environment

Hot Bean Dip

Makes 15 Servings

1 (16 ounce) can refried beans
1 (8 ounce) package cream cheese, softened
1 (8 ounce) carton sour cream
2 tablespoons taco seasoning,
   from a taco mix package
6 drops Tabasco sauce
¼ cup onion, chopped
¾ cup Monterey Jack cheese, grated
¾ cup Cheddar cheese, grated
1 bag nacho chips

Preheat oven to 350°F. Mix the beans, cream cheese, sour cream, taco seasoning, Tabasco, and onion together in a baking dish. Spread the cheeses over the top and bake, uncovered, 15–20 minutes. Once the dip has heated through and the cheese has melted, serve with nacho chips.

This dish is a great alternative to the traditional seven-layer dip. Plus, pinto beans are a great source of fiber (helps lower cholesterol and prevent heart disease), vitamin B1 (good for your memory), iron (increases energy), and protein.

THE AUDUBON INN

Our sixteen elegantly appointed rooms offer comfort and romance. Each room includes private double whirlpool baths, custom-made queen-size four-poster beds, Scottish Lace curtains, and sitting area. Suites include DVD and CD players, and refrigerator in the parlor. The Audubon Inn is also home to Morgan's Restaurant, an extraordinary restaurant that features fresh, regional American cuisine prepared on site, attentive service, and a beautiful atmosphere. Specials and homemade soups are prepared daily by our executive chef. Also found at The Audubon is A.J.'s Pub. Relax in the laid-back atmosphere and enjoy great food and fantastic drinks.

All of our guests enjoy a complimentary continental-plus breakfast, which consists of bagels, muffins, coffee cakes, hot and cold cereal, yogurt, and fresh fruits, as well as hot and cold beverages.

INNKEEPERS: Michael & Stacy Shewey
ADDRESS: 45 N. Main St, Mayville, WI 53050
TELEPHONE: (920) 387-5858
E-MAIL: info@auduboninn.com
WEBSITE: www.auduboninn.com
ROOMS: 16 Rooms
CHILDREN: Welcome
PETS: Pet-free environment

Wisconsin Cheddar Cheese & Beer Soup

Makes 2 Gallons

8 ounces vegetable oil	2 ounces garlic, minced
12 ounces flour	12 ounces beer
1½ gallons chicken stock	4 pounds Tillamook
¼ pound popcorn	Cheddar cheese, grated
2 ounces butter	1 ounce dry mustard
1 pound onion, minced	1 pint heavy cream
1 pound mushrooms, quartered	Tabasco sauce, to taste
1 pound celery, small dice	Worcestershire sauce, to taste
1 pound carrots, small dice	Salt and pepper, to taste

Combine the oil and flour to make a blond roux and cook in a heavy-bottomed saucepan over medium-high heat for 12 minutes. Gradually add the stock, whisking constantly to work out any lumps. Simmer 45 minutes, or until the soup has a good flavor and a velvety texture. Strain through a chinoise. Prepare the popcorn and reserve for service. Heat the butter over medium-high and add the onions, mushrooms, celery, carrots, and garlic. Sweat the vegetables until cooked halfway; set aside.

Return the soup to a simmer. Whisk in the beer and cheese. Continue to heat the soup until the cheese has melted, but do not boil. Blend the dry mustard with enough water to make a paste. Add the mustard mixture and the cream to the soup and bring back to a simmer. Season with Tabasco, Worcestershire, salt, and pepper to taste. 30 minutes before service, add the vegetables to the soup. Keep the soup warming over very low temperature, or pour into a soup warmer. Serve in warmed soup cups topped with popcorn.

EARTH RIDER HOTEL

Earth Rider is a bike-themed boutique hotel located in a completely restored building in Brodhead's downtown historic business district. Each of Earth Rider's five rooms is named after one of the 5-time winners of the Tour de France, the world's greatest bicycle race. Although each room features unique bicycle themed elements, you need not be a cyclist to reward yourself with its quiet restfulness. Each room features a private designer bath, pillow-top mattress, and luxury linens.

The property is Travel Green Wisconsin certified and has adopted many environmentally friendly practices including extensive recycling, natural cleaning supplies, a rain barrel, dispensers for amenities,

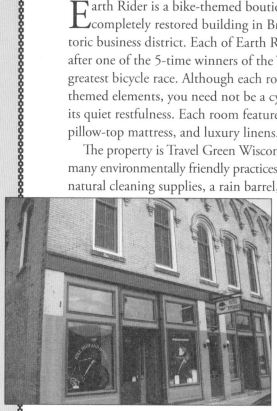

reused bicycle parts as stylish furniture and fixtures, and encouragement for the ultimate eco-friendly form of transportation — pedal power! Cycling the Sugar River Trail, Badger Trail, and quiet backroads is supported by a full-service bike shop on the first floor where bicycle rentals are available for all ages. Wisconsin is second in the United States for cycling, so let Earth Rider Hotel be your base for exploring the pastoral sights and diverse communities of South Central Wisconsin at the human speed of a bicycle.

INNKEEPER: Sharon Kaminecki
ADDRESS: 929 W Exchange Street, Brodhead, WI 53520
TELEPHONE: (608) 897-8300; (866) 245-5276
E-MAIL: info@earthridercycling.com
WEBSITE: www.earthridercycling.com
ROOMS: 5 Rooms
CHILDREN: Welcome
PETS: Inquire

Four Day Chili

Makes 10 Servings

*"This chili won first prize in the non-traditional category
at the Oktoberfest Chili Contest in Brodhead, WI, in 2004,
2005, 2006, 2007, and 2008. It is considered non-traditional
because of the use of steak."*

—INNKEEPER, *Earth Rider Hotel*

1 pound round steak
½ cup Jim Beam, or Jack Daniels
4 cloves garlic, minced
4 tablespoons Worcestershire sauce
¼ cup olive oil
1 handful wood chips, hickory preferred
3 poblano peppers
1–2 jalapeno peppers
2 large tomatoes,
    or 1 (16 ounce) can diced tomatoes
1 large onion, coarsely sliced
1 large red bell pepper, coarsely sliced
1 large green bell pepper, coarsely sliced
1 pound ground pork or turkey
1 (12 ounce) bottle Guinness extra stout
2 cans tomato paste
1 (16 ounce) can free-range chicken broth
3 tablespoons Mexican oregano
3 bay leaves
Kosher salt, to taste
2 tablespoons cumin seeds
¼ teaspoon each white and
    black pepper, freshly ground
1 (16 ounce) can red kidney beans
1 (16 ounce) can black beans
1 pint ice cream, your favorite flavor

Day one (pre-preparation): Marinate the steak overnight: Place in a non-reactive, tightly covered container or Ziploc bag, with the whiskey, 2 cloves garlic, Worcestershire sauce, and half the olive oil. Turn end over end several times throughout the night. Soak the wood chips in water.

Day two (cooking): Heat a charcoal grill. Once the grill is hot, toss in some of the wood chips, or wrap the wood chips in foil, punch holes in the foil, and place directly over the coals. Roast and rotate the poblanos and jalapenos over the smoky fire until the skins loosen, about 10 minutes, turning so they don't catch fire. Once they're roasted, place them in a covered pot to self-steam for about 15 minutes to help loosen the skin. Grill the steaks over the smoky charcoal fire until rare. They will be cooked again in the stockpot.

Preheat oven to 350°F. Par-boil the tomatoes in a large pot of boiling water, about 1–2 minutes a piece. Peel the skins off and coarsely chop the tomatoes. Place the chopped tomatoes on a cookie sheet and roast 20–25 minutes, until some of the liquid is gone but the tomatoes are not totally dried out or burnt. If using canned tomatoes, roast per above. Place the roasted tomatoes in a large (at least 6 quarts) stock pot. Remove the skins, seeds, and stems from the poblanos and jalapenos. Place the poblanos in a blender with ¼ cup water and blend until very fine. Blend the jalapenos separately.

Heat the remaining oil in a large skillet over medium-low flame. Cook the remaining garlic until fragrant and then add the onion and bell peppers. Increase heat to medium-high and cook several minutes, or until onions are almost clear but not caramelized (the bell peppers should still be firm). Add the ground pork and cook until browned, skim the fat if necessary. Season with pepper and add to the stock pot with the tomatoes, but do not heat yet.

Trim and the fat from the steak and discard. Cut into ¼x¼x1-inch strips. Add the beef to the stock pot. Add the beer, tomato paste, chicken stock, and oregano. Turn heat to medium-low making sure not to boil the chili or the steak will dry out. Place the bay leaves in a tea ball and add to the stockpot — this will make it easier to remove when done.

Toast the cumin seeds in a dry pan for 2–3 minutes until a bit darkened and fragrant. Remove from heat and cool enough to place in a plastic bag. Beat the seeds until powdered; add to the stock pot along with the poblano purée. Heat the chili almost to a boil then lower heat to a simmer so that the meat doesn't dry out. Stir occasionally and taste to balance spices. Add the pepper and simmer 30 minutes. Taste and add jalapeno purée to desired heat. Drain the beans and add to the pot. Cook about 30 more minutes, until the peppers are softened, stirring carefully to avoid breaking the beans. Remove the bay leaves. It's ok to serve the chili at this point, but flavor will be better if you cover and refrigerate overnight.

Day three (mellowing): Reheat the chili gently, (the microwave is ok), and eat topped with raw chopped onions, grated Cheddar cheese, and oyster crackers. If you are serving on a buffet, keep the temperature around 125°F. This temperature is hot enough to eat right away and does not dry out the meat.

Important: When done eating chili, eat some ice cream.

Day four (payment): Some time today, you will be saying, "Come on ice cream, come on ice cream." Just kidding.

This is an original recipe that has been refined over twenty-five years and is copyrighted, R.M. Kaminecki 2008. Any reproduction must be clearly cited to the author.

Tips and Variations

This is a mild chili and anyone who wishes is spicier can add hot sauce to taste. Adding more poblanos will add more flavor than heat. To thicken, leave out the chicken broth or blend a half can of beans before adding to the mixture… And yes, you can cook this in one day as long as you marinade the meat the night before.

SCHUSTER MANSION

Built in 1891, this captivating mansion, once known as the "Red Castle," stands with majesty and grace. Innkeepers Laura Sue and Rick hope to bring this mansion back to what it may have been in its heyday.

Come to a place where your hosts are patiently waiting for your arrival. As you enter the foyer, you are drawn in with a feeling of warmth and calmness. A sense of home invites you inside and you'll find that you've left all the pressures of life at the door. Each of the five calming guest rooms features its own unique décor and color scheme and our "famous" cookies are waiting for you in the Butler's Pantry. So come and relax at the charming and historic Schuster Mansion.

INNKEEPERS:	Laura Sue & Rick Mosier
ADDRESS:	3209 W Wells Street, Milwaukee, WI 53208
TELEPHONE:	(414) 342-3210
E-MAIL:	welcome@schustermansion.com
WEBSITE:	www.schustermansion.com
ROOMS:	5 Rooms; Private & shared baths
CHILDREN:	Inquire
PETS:	Resident pets only

Mushroom Bisque

Makes 4-6 Servings

"This recipe was adapted from the November/December 2007 Victoria Magazine."

—INNKEEPER, *Schuster Mansion*

MUSHROOM STOCK

2 tablespoons extra-virgin olive oil
1 cup chopped onion
½ cup chopped carrots
½ cup chopped celery
1 tablespoon minced garlic
2 cups dried mushroom blend
4 cups chicken stock

MUSHROOM BISQUE

1 tablespoon extra-virgin
   olive oil
1 cup sliced leeks
1 tablespoon minced garlic
1⅓ cups chopped
   baby bella mushrooms
2 cups mushroom stock
1 teaspoon lemon zest
1 tablespoon lemon juice
2 cups heavy cream
⅛ cup dry white wine
¼ cup butter
1 teaspoon fresh chopped thyme

To make the stock: Heat the olive oil in a large stockpot over medium-high heat. Add the onion, carrot, celery, and garlic and cook until they begin to soften (about 4 minutes). Add the remaining ingredients and simmer over medium heat for about 15 minutes. Strain and discard solids.

For the bisque: Heat the olive oil in a large stockpot over medium-high heat. Add the leeks, garlic, and mushrooms and cook until the mushrooms begin to brown (about 5 minutes). Add the 2 cups of stock and bring to a simmer. Whisk in the lemon zest and juice, cream, and wine. Add the butter and thyme and simmer over medium heat for about 6 minutes. Garnish with sautéed mushrooms and lemon ribbons to serve.

BAY POINT INN

At Bay Point Inn, guests will enjoy spectacular water views punctuated with the islands of Green Bay and framed by pristine woodlands. The inn offers spacious one-bedroom accommodations with luxurious interior décor. Outside, guests will find luscious gardens that mirror the magnificence of a European vacation villa.

Bay Point Inn is the ultimate vacation experience in Door County, complete with the designer furnishings, Italian porcelain tile baths, Gilchrist & Soames bath amenities, Hydro-Thermo massage whirlpools, a gourmet breakfast buffet, pools overlooking the shoreline, and many romantic enhancements.

INNKEEPERS: Myles Dannhausen

ADDRESS: 7933 State Highway 42, Egg Harbor, WI 54209

TELEPHONE: (800) 707-6660

E-MAIL: stay@baypointinn.com

WEBSITE: www.baypointinn.com

ROOMS: 10 Rooms

CHILDREN: Inquire

PETS: Pet-free environment

Peanut Stew

Makes 8 Servings

"Our innkeeper, Myles Dannhausen, developed a menu of African specialties while he was a Peace Corps volunteer in Sierra Leone. Once home, Myles introduced his family and friends to African cuisine. Peanut stew is a main course and is a fricassee of chicken and/or meat, flavored and thickened with tomato purée and peanut butter. It may be served with white rice, or with skewered chicken/beef."

—*INNKEEPER, Bay Point Inn*

1 stewing chicken, cut into pieces
1 pound round steak, cut into cubes
2 small onions, chopped
2 small hot peppers, freshly ground
4 cups water
½ cup tomato purée
½ cup peanut butter
Salt and pepper
Cayenne pepper
Oregano

Place the cut up chicken, beef cubes, onion, and pepper in a large stew pot with a lid. Add water and 1 teaspoon salt. Cover and simmer until the meat and the chicken are tender. Stir in the tomato purée and peanut butter and simmer 20 minutes. Add the seasonings to taste. Serve over plain or Jollof rice.

> *Jollof rice is a one-pot rice dish from Africa that includes ingredients like onions, tomatoes, spices, and sometimes vegetables and meat.*

GREEN FOUNTAIN INN

This unique Waupaca inn located in the heart of town, features four individually themed guest rooms and is perfect for private dinner parties, small weddings and receptions, showers, anniversary and birthday parties, and even murder mystery dinners.

In addition to its restaurant kitchen, the inn is also home to the Secret Garden Café and the Back Door Bakery. The Café is located on the first floor of the inn and serves lunches Tuesday through Saturday. Menus vary from day to day and feature seasonal foods from local farmers when available. All foods including soups, artisan breads, grilled sandwiches, and fabulous desserts are prepared from scratch. The Back Door Bakery is open seasonally; wedding and

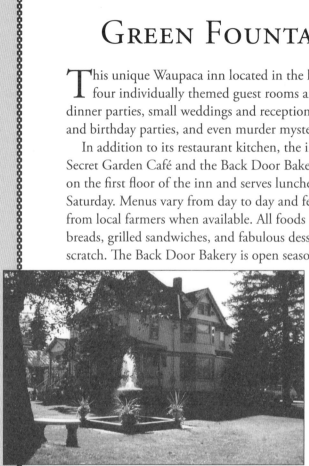

birthday cakes and homemade breads can be special ordered. Cakes are made with butter, no hydrogenated fats or oils, natural ingredients and flavorings and are decorated with fresh flowers.

INNKEEPER:	Cindy Oerter
ADDRESS:	604 S Main Street, Waupaca, WI 54981
TELEPHONE:	(715) 258-5171; (800) 603-4600
E-MAIL:	greenfountaininn@yahoo.com
WEBSITE:	www.greenfountaininn.com
ROOMS:	4 Rooms
CHILDREN:	Inquire
PETS:	Pet-free environment

Italian Basil Tomato Soup

Makes 4 Servings

1 pound Italian sausage

1 medium onion, chopped

2 stalks celery, chopped

2 (14.5 ounce) cans diced Italian tomatoes

1 (8 ounce) small can tomato sauce

¼ cup basil, chopped

½ cup lemon juice

2 tablespoons sugar

1 tablespoon Worcestershire sauce

1 teaspoon salt

¾ teaspoon hot sauce

Heat a bit of oil in a sauté heavy-bottomed soup pot over medium-high heat. Remove the sausage from its casings and crumble into the pot. Add the onion and celery and cook until the meat is browned and the vegetables are tender. Add in the tomatoes and purée together using a blender (regular or immersion). Add the tomato sauce, basil, lemon juice, sugar, Worcestershire sauce, salt, and hot sauce and reduce heat to low. Cook just until heated through. Garnish with grated Parmesan cheese and/or croutons.

Tips and Variations

Italian sausage comes in either sweet or hot varieties. Use either one or a combination of both.

Curried Carrot Soup

Makes 4 Servings

2 teaspoons sesame oil

1 large onion, chopped

5 cups vegetable broth

4 carrots, chopped

1½ teaspoons curry powder

1 teaspoon thyme

1 bay leaf

3 ounces cream cheese

5 tablespoons fresh parsley

Dash of cayenne pepper

Heat the oil in a heavy-bottomed soup pot over medium-high heat. Sauté the onion. Once the onion is cooked, add the broth, carrots, curry, thyme, and bay leaf to the pot. Bring to a boil and then reduce to a simmer. Cook until the carrots are tender. Remove the bay leaf and purée the soup using a blender (regular or immersion).* Add the cream cheese and parsley and heat until the cheese has melted into the soup. Serve.

Tips and Variations

*If using a regular blender to purée the soup, blend in batches as the heat may cause the lid to loosen. An immersion blender is best as you can use it right in the pot.

Broccoli Craisin Salad

Makes 6 Servings

*"We have a café in our inn where we have lunch from
11–2, Monday–Friday. We always have homemade soups,
paninis as our homemade breads, and mouth watering desserts.
We also have cooking classes where we share our favorite recipes."*

—INNKEEPER, *Green Fountain Inn*

3 heads broccoli
1 small red onion, chopped
½ cup Craisins
½ cup mayonnaise
Juice of ½ a lemon
1 tablespoon sugar
Salt and pepper, to taste
½ cup roasted and salted sunflower seeds,
   (optional)

Wash and chop the broccoli. Place in a bowl with the red onion
and toss together. In a small bowl, combine the Craisins, mayonnaise, lemon juice, sugar, salt, and pepper. Add the sunflower
seeds and toss with the broccoli/onion mixture.

OLD RITTENHOUSE INN

Already well known as a summer/fall destination, the Rittenhouse Inn has strived for many years to encourage quiet-season business in Bayfield by offering packages and special events like the Wassail luncheon and dinner concerts throughout the holiday season. The Inn also offers wine tasting and murder mystery weekends during the winter and spring months. Whether guests are planning for quiet relaxation or an active vacation adventure, staff is on-hand to make them feel at home.

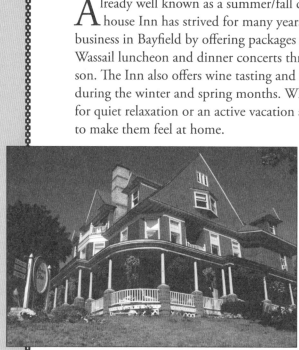

The 301 Rittenhouse Restaurant is open to the public for breakfast and dinner year-round and features regional cuisine prepared with gourmet artistry and the finest local ingredients. Lunch is offered June–September.

INNKEEPERS:	Jerry & Mary Phillips, Mark & Wendy Phillips
ADDRESS:	301 Rittenhouse Avenue, Bayfield, WI 54814
TELEPHONE:	(715) 779-5111; (800) 799-2129
E-MAIL:	gourmet@rittenhouseinn.com
WEBSITE:	www.rittenhouseinn.com
ROOMS:	20 Rooms
CHILDREN:	Inquire
PETS:	Pet-free environment

Lake Superior Smoked Trout Salad

Makes 6 Servings

DRESSING

3 cups mayonnaise

½ cup fresh squeezed lemon juice

¼ cup prepared horseradish

¼ cup ketchup

1 tablespoon paprika

2 tablespoons chopped fresh parsley

2 tablespoons chopped fresh dill

1 teaspoon minced fresh garlic

SALAD

8 ounces mixed greens

1½ cups prepared wild rice, chilled

1 cup or ½ pound smoked lake trout,
    boned and flaked

4 ounces aged Wisconsin Cheddar,
    cubed or crumbled

¾ cup prepared dressing (recipe above)

½ red onion, thinly sliced

Sea salt and fresh ground pepper, to taste

¼ cup shopped fresh chives, parsley, or dill

For the dressing: Mix all of the ingredients well. Chill, reserving ¾ cup to toss with the salad ingredients and refrigerate the remainder.

For the salad: In a large bowl, gently toss all of the ingredients except the fresh herb leaves; reserve a bit of the Cheddar. Refrigerate remaining dressing for later use. Season to taste. Divide between six plates and garnish with remaining cheese and fresh herbs.

Optional garnishes: soft-poached or hard-boiled egg, sun gold cherry tomatoes, or bacon.

Honeybee Inn B&B

Pure indulgence and luxury is yours when you reserve a room at the Honeybee Inn Bed & Breakfast.

Your hosts, Barbara and Fred Ruka, invite you to come and be immersed in pure luxury and impeccably clean accommodations! Deluxe whirlpools, body jet showers, fireplaces, a huge video library, chocolates on your pillow, luxury spa robes and linens, down comforters, and feather beds are just a few of our great amenities! Our rooms are large, comfortable, spotless, and beautifully appointed with the finest amenities. And our breakfasts have taken on a legendary status among inn goers!

Honeybee Inn is located just a short drive from Milwaukee, Madison, Oshkosh, and Fond du Lac. The inn is also a mere walk

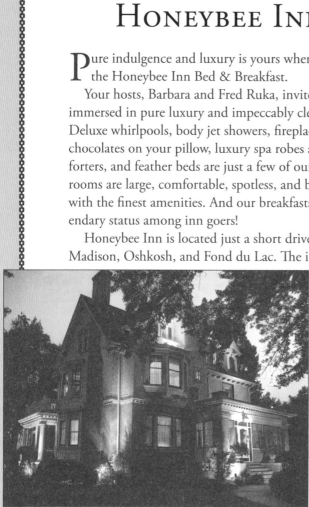

from Horicon Marsh, the birding mecca of the Midwest! So whether you are canoeing or birding at the Horicon Marsh, hiking or biking the Wild Goose State Trail, skiing down the slopes, or shopping at the nearby huge antique mall, there is something for everyone.

INNKEEPERS:	Barbara & Fred Ruka
ADDRESS:	611 E Walnut Street, Horicon, WI 53032
TELEPHONE:	(920) 485-4855
E-MAIL:	innkeeper@honeybeeinn.com
WEBSITE:	www.honeybeeinn.com
ROOMS:	4 Rooms
CHILDREN:	Children age 12 and older welcome
PETS:	Resident pets only

Frog Eye Salad

Makes 12 Servings

"We have been making this salad for probably 25 years now. Whenever I ask my kids what to make for a special dinner, this is the first thing out of their mouths."

—INNKEEPER, *Honeybee Inn B&B*

¾ cup sugar

2 tablespoons flour

½ teaspoon salt

²/₃ cup pineapple juice

1 egg

1 teaspoon lemon juice

1 cup acini de pepi pasta

2 cans mandarin oranges, drained

1 (20 ounce) can pineapple tidbits, drained

1 (8 ounce) container Cool Whip

1 cup mini marshmallows

1 (20 ounce) can crushed pineapple, drained

In a small saucepan over medium heat, mix together the sugar, flour, and salt. Stir in the pineapple juice and egg. Cook, stirring constantly, until thickened. Add the lemon juice and set aside. Cook the pasta and stir into the pineapple juice mixture. Let cool in the refrigerator. Add the remaining ingredients and cool before serving.

Chicken Pasta Fruit Salad

Makes 6 Servings

*"This has to be one of the best chicken salad recipes in existence.
It has a very different twist with the tortellini in it."*
—INNKEEPER, *Honeybee Inn B&B*

1½ pounds cooked chicken breast, diced
3 cups seedless grapes, halved
2 cups pea pods, steamed 1 minute or less
12 ounces cheese tortellini, cooked
1 large cucumber, peeled, seeded,
   and diced (optional)
3 diced green onions
½ cup Craisins or raisins
½ cup diced celery

DRESSING
½ cup mayonnaise
½ cup shredded Parmesan cheese
¼ cup lemon juice
2 tablespoons sugar
Salt and pepper, to taste
4 tablespoons fresh parsley, chopped
2 teaspoons fresh thyme, or 1 teaspoon dried

Toasted almonds for garnish

In a large bowl, combine the chicken, grapes, pea pods, tortellini, cucumber, green onions, Craisins, and celery. In a separate medium bowl, combine the dressing ingredients and mix well. Pour the dressing over the salad and chill. Serve garnished with almonds if desired.

Breakfast Potatoes

Makes 6 Servings

4 cups diced potatoes
½ cup diced onion
¼ cup butter, melted
1½ cup cooked bacon, chopped
½ cup flour
3 cups milk
1 cup shredded Cheddar cheese
4 teaspoons garlic salt
¼ teaspoon pepper
½ teaspoon salt

Preheat oven to 350°F. Cook the diced potatoes. Dice the onion and place in a skillet with the butter; sauté. Add the bacon to the skillet and cook for 2 minutes. Add the flour and stir in to make a paste. Cook 5 minutes before adding the milk. Stir until all of the lumps are gone. Cook the mixture for 10 minutes and continue stirring. Add the potatoes, cheese, and seasonings. Mix until the cheese is melted. Place the potatoes in one layer on a cookie sheet or in a baking dish and bake 10 minutes. Can be made ahead of time and warmed up to serve.

ARBOR INN

Perched on a bluff in the quaint town of Prescott, Wisconsin, and located in a reclusive and quiet cul-de-sac sits The Arbor Inn. Built in 1902, this B&B has a St. Croix River view. The home proudly boasts its age with a fieldstone foundation, hardwood floors, exterior wood columns, and a wood-burning fireplace that accentuates the living room.

Guests are invited to help themselves to hot beverages and fresh homemade goodies throughout the day. In-house massage services are available and highly recommended as guests visit to rest, relax and rejuvenate. Outside, seasonal grapevine covered porches magically melt hours away.

In town, guests will find great antique shops, riverfront restaurants, and unique pubs. Prescott is also home to a railroad lift bridge and drawbridge that are both spectacular sights to see.

INNKEEPERS: John & Deb Sherman
ADDRESS: 434 N Court Street, Prescott, WI 54021
TELEPHONE: (715) 262-2222; (888) 262-1090
E-MAIL: relax@thearborinn.com
WEBSITE: www.thearborinn.com
ROOMS: 4 Rooms
CHILDREN: Inquire
PETS: Inquire

Sausage & Potato Breakfast Casserole

Makes 4-6 Servings

"The breakfast sausage casserole is a favorite with guests and is one of our most requested recipes. When any of our four children return home, it is one of the staples of the visit — they would be disappointed to leave without having some!"

—INNKEEPER, *Arbor Inn*

1 pound breakfast sausage
2 tablespoons flour
1½ cups milk, not lowfat
1 (1 pound) package frozen hash browns
4 green onions, finely chopped
1¼ cups grated sharp Cheddar cheese

Preheat oven to 350°F and butter an 8-inch square baking dish. In a heated skillet over medium-high heat, cook the sausage until brown. Do not drain the sausage. Mix in the flour and then the milk and cook until the mixture thickens and comes to a boil. Arrange the potatoes in the prepared dish and top (in layers) with the green onions, 1 cup of cheese, ⅓ of the green onions, the sausage mixture, and the remaining ¼ cup cheese. Bake 45 minutes. Sprinkle with the remaining green onion.

Tips and Variations

Deb and John usually serve this dish as a main course with a side of fruit or tomatoes, but it also makes a great accompaniment for most egg and omelet entrées.

COOKSVILLE
FARMHOUSE INN

Cooksville Farmhouse Inn is conveniently located between Madison and Janesville, near Stoughton, Evansville, and Edgerton. The farmhouse, originally built around 1845, is on the

National Registry of Historic Places, along with most of the village. Cooksville is a small, rural community of 35 houses that has a rich history.

The inn borders a lovely restored prairie crisscrossed by paths for walks beside the spring-fed stream in the summer and snow-shoeing in the winter. Enjoy the quiet, rustic, family-friendly atmosphere of the farmhouse, which has a soapstone wood-stove and massive freestanding fireplace to keep guests cozy when the snow flies. Guests will also love the great views of the prairie and sunsets.

INNKEEPERS: Bob & Martha Degner

ADDRESS: 11203 N State Road 138, Evansville, WI 53536

TELEPHONE: (608) 335-8375

E-MAIL: relax@cooksvillefarmhouseinn.com

WEBSITE: www.cooksvillefarmhouseinn.com

ROOMS: 4 Rooms; Private and shared baths

CHILDREN: Welcome

PETS: Inquire

Martha's Breakfast Corn Bake

Makes 8 Servings

2 cups corn meal

2 teaspoons baking powder

1 teaspoon salt

1 cup yogurt

1 (16 ounce) can creamed corn

¼ cup olive oil

¼ cup melted butter or margarine

2 cups frozen whole kernel corn

1½–2 cups grated Cheddar cheese

Preheat oven to 350°F and grease two 9-inch pie pans. In a medium bowl, combine the corn meal, baking powder, and salt. In a large bowl, combine the yogurt, creamed corn, oil, butter, and whole kernel corn. Add the dry ingredients to the wet mixture. Divide the batter evenly between the pans and sprinkle with cheese. Bake 40–45 minutes.

Tips and Variations

This Corn Bake makes a great side dish to any meal. Try adding a can of Ro-Tel tomatoes for a kicked up, spicy version with dinner.

INN AT
LONESOME HOLLOW

Our Inn is situated on 160 acres of mostly wooded rural land near Soldiers Grove, in the Driftless Area of southwest Wisconsin. Our Kickapoo Valley B&B lies between La Crosse and Prairie du Chien. We offer four miles of private hiking trails and

our skies are completely free of light pollution so the stargazing is superb.

We have three deluxe rooms in the main house, a two-bedroom cabin, and a separate house with two very private suites. Full country breakfasts using organic and locally grown ingredients are served family-style each morning. Breakfasts are complemented by raspberry and wild blackberry jams, prepared using berries picked from our gardens and woods, and maple syrup produced from our own trees.

INNKEEPERS:	Nora & Pete Knapik
ADDRESS:	15415 Vance Road, Soldiers Grove, WI 54655
TELEPHONE:	(608) 624-3429
E-MAIL:	info@lonesomehollow.com
WEBSITE:	www.lonesomehollow.com
ROOMS:	3 Rooms; 2 Suites; 1 Cabin
CHILDREN:	Inquire
PETS:	Inquire

Savory Spinach Bread Pudding with Mushrooms & Sausage

Plan ahead, this dish needs to be refrigerated overnight!

Makes 6 Servings

"A good friend gave us this recipe when she found out we were opening a b&b. Over the years, we adjusted the ingredients to be sure the bread pudding was just moist enough. If serving vegetarian guests, the sausage can be omitted. It is still just as delicious."

—INNKEEPER, *Inn at Lonesome Hollow*

4 ounces sliced baby bella mushrooms
½ tablespoon olive oil
3 cups seasoned croutons
1 pound bulk pork sausage
4 eggs
2 cups milk
¼ teaspoon dry mustard
1 can cream of mushroom soup
10 ounces frozen spinach,
     thawed and drained, or ¾ pound fresh, wilted
1 cup shredded sharp Cheddar cheese,
     reserve ⅛ cup
1 cup shredded Monterey Jack cheese,
     reserve ⅛ cup

Sauté the sliced mushrooms in the olive oil and set aside. Spread the croutons on the bottom of a buttered 13x9-inch baking dish. Crumble and cook the sausage; drain. Spread the sausage over the croutons. In a medium bowl, whisk together the eggs and milk. Stir in the dry mustard, soup, mushrooms, spinach, and cheeses. Pour the mixture over the croutons and sausage. Cover and refrigerate overnight.

The following morning: Preheat oven to 325°F and bake, uncovered, for 50 minutes, until set and lightly browned. Remove from oven and sprinkle with reserved cheeses. Return to the oven for an additional 5 minutes, or until melted.

Luncheon & Dinner Entrées

Luncheon & Dinner Entrées

*Might we suggest a
Wisconsin micro-brew served in a
frosty mug, or a fine Wisconsin wine
with overtones of fruits and spices,
to accompany these main dishes?*

KINNI CREEK LODGE & OUTFITTERS

Enjoy the rustic simplicity of Kinni Creek Lodge, a cozy year-round retreat setting nestled near whispering woods and privately located along the Kinnickinnic, a Class 1 trout stream in River Falls, Wisconsin. This quiet and secluded inn, located just off Main street, caters to summer vacationers interested in bird watching, fly fishing, hiking, biking, kayaking, or relaxing. In the winter, cross-country ski or snowmobile trails are just minutes from the inn!

Kinni Creek features three rooms, each named for areas of the Kinnickinnic River: Rocky Branch, Pete's Creek, and Lower Dam. Each room is outfitted with log furniture and a fireplace so you can relax in a cozy "Northwoods" atmosphere, or enjoy fly-fishing right outside! Next door in the Ice House enjoy beverages and munchies while playing with games or puzzles.

INNKEEPER: Paige Olson

ADDRESS: 545 N Main Street, River Falls, WI 54022

TELEPHONE: (715) 425-7378; (877) 504-9705

E-MAIL: guide@kinnicreek.com

WEBSITE: www.kinnicreek.com

ROOMS: 3 Rooms; 1 Cabin

CHILDREN: Welcome

PETS: Inquire

Trout a la Kinni

Makes 2–6 Servings

2–6 trout
Garllc
1 medium onion, diced
Butter
Salt and pepper, to taste
Capers or chives
1 lemon, sliced

Clean the entrails out of the trout and prepare whole. Stuff the garlic, onion, butter, salt, and pepper into the fish. Place the fish on a piece of tinfoil and grill on medium heat, five minutes on each side, until golden brown. Garnish with capers or chives and serve with a slice of lemon.

Tips and Variations

For a hearty fisherman's breakfast, serve with scrambled eggs, American fries, and toast.

OLD RITTENHOUSE INN

The Rittenhouse Inn is a country inn and gourmet restaurant with twenty guest rooms in three historic Bayfield homes. Most rooms feature a fireplace, whirlpool tub, and scenic views of Lake Superior.

The Inn was created by Jerry and Mary Phillips, former music teachers from Madison, who fell in love with the "big red house on the hill." The couple's first big break occurred in 1985, when Jerry's cheesecake appeared on the cover of *Gourmet* magazine. "The phone started ringing and didn't stop for a year," says Mary.

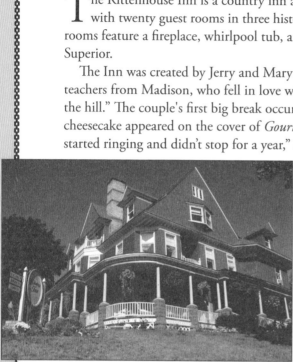

The 301 Rittenhouse Restaurant serves a five-course dinner showcasing the regional harvest with creative appetizers, soups, salads, entrées, and desserts. In addition, the Inn is open for breakfast year-round, and lunch from June to September.

INNKEEPERS:	Jerry & Mary Phillips, Mark & Wendy Phillips
ADDRESS:	301 Rittenhouse Avenue, Bayfield, WI 54814
TELEPHONE:	(715) 779-5111; (800) 799-2129
E-MAIL:	gourmet@rittenhouseinn.com
WEBSITE:	www.rittenhouseinn.com
ROOMS:	20 Rooms
CHILDREN:	Inquire
PETS:	Pet-free environment

Fresh Lake Trout
with Rittenhouse Reddening

Makes 8 Servings

8 ounces bread crumbs

½ cup dry dill, chopped

3 tablespoons garlic powder

1 tablespoon salt

½ cup Old Rittenhouse Reddening*
   (see recipe below)

4 pounds fresh trout filets

½ cup butter

SAUCE

½ pound softened butter

1 tablespoon minced fresh garlic

2 tablespoons Reddening

½ cup tomato paste

½ teaspoon Tabasco

Using a food processor, blend together the bread crumbs, dill, garlic powder, salt, and Rittenhouse reddening. Cover the flesh side of the fish with the crumb mixture. Melt the butter in a large skillet and place the filets skin-side-down over the butter. Cover and cook until the fish flakes. Remove the filets from the pan and remove the skin. Serve on warm plates with sauce on the side.

For the sauce: In a food processor fitted with a steel blade, process the softened butter, fresh garlic, reddening, tomato paste, and Tabasco

*For the Rittenhouse Reddening: Blend together 1 part curry, 1 part white pepper, 1 part cayenne pepper, 2 parts onion powder, 3 parts garlic powder, and 6 parts paprika. Store in a tightly covered container in a dry place.

ENCHANTED VALLEY B&B

A Piece of Heaven...

The secluded Enchanted Valley Bed & Breakfast, nestled in the beautiful rolling hills and valleys of rural Cross Plains, lies on five acres of lush woods and open fields. Our home is a soothing, yet energizing certified Feng Shui space. Window walls and a cathedral ceiling incorporate structure with nature, and likewise, body with soul. Heavenly feather queen beds, a wood burning stove or bonfire for cool nights, a bountiful garden, gourmet vegan breakfasts, and decks to enjoy breathtaking panoramic views ensure reveling "in the moment."

A concert of singing birds beckons you each morning from the patio door in your bedroom to your private deck. As you stroll through Ken and Marcia's numerous organically grown vegetable, herb, and flower gardens, listen to the many species of birds they attract to their paradise. The Jacuzzi, therapeutic massage, Reiki master teaching, outside cedar sauna, labyrinth, and naturopathy, iridology, and "mindfulness," (i.e. Thich Nhat Hanh) conversations make your stay an everlasting one.

INNKEEPERS: Kenneth & Marcia Helgerson
ADDRESS: 5554 Enchanted Valley Road, Cross Plains, WI 53528
TELEPHONE: (608) 798-4554
E-MAIL: serenity@enchantedvalley.com
WEBSITE: www.enchantedvalley.com
ROOMS: 2 Rooms
CHILDREN: Inquire
PETS: Pet-free environment

Salmon Loaf

Makes 4 Servings

½ cup salad dressing
1 can cream of celery soup
2 eggs, beaten
½ cup chopped onion
½ cup chopped green pepper
1 teaspoon lemon juice
16 ounces salmon
1 cup bread crumbs, plain

Preheat oven to 350°F. In a large bowl, combine the dressing soup, and eggs. Add in the onion, peppers, and juice and mix well. Toss the salmon lightly in the bread crumbs and combine with the other ingredients. Place the mixture in a greased loaf pan and bake 1 hour.

Tips and Variations

Use canned, boneless and skinless salmon in this dish for a quick timesaver.

SABAMBA ALPACA RANCH & B&B

Our 1890 remodeled farmstead home is a family-friendly b&b that welcomes all visitors. The home is filled with maple and hickory wood floors, and the antique mantel in the guest living space is breathtaking.

Each guest room comes with comfy robes. Rosie's Room has a wonderful whirlpool tub and pillow-top bed that you won't want to leave and Lori's Room has a cozy fireplace. Enjoy breakfast in your room or in the dining room and watch the alpaca in the pasture. After, you can help with the daily care of the alpaca, or relax on the wrap-around porch and read a book or listen to music.

INNKEEPERS: Tom & Sally Schmidt

ADDRESS: 2338 Hickory Road, De Pere, WI 54115

TELEPHONE: (920) 371-0003

E-MAIL: sschmidt@sabambaalpaca.com

WEBSITE: www.sabambaalpaca.com

ROOMS: 2 Rooms

CHILDREN: Welcome

PETS: Resident pets only

Pork Loin with Coriander & Garlic Crust

Makes 4-6 Servings

*"This dish is inspired by Elizabeth David
who makes a coriander crust for lamb and
by a dish made at the Heathman Hotel in Portland."*
—INNKEEPER, *Sabamba Alpaca Ranch and B&B*

¼ cup coriander seeds
1 cup fresh bread crumbs
2 large cloves garlic, peeled
½ teaspoon salt
¼ cup extra virgin olive oil, more if needed
1 boneless pork loin (2¼ pound)
Freshly ground pepper
½ cup water

Preheat oven to 400°F. Crush the coriander seeds in a food processor for about 30 seconds. Add the bread crumbs and garlic and process to combine. With the processor running, add the salt and ¼ cup olive oil and process just until mixture is combined. Mixture should be moist enough to hold lightly together when pressed. If not, add another tablespoon of oil and continue adding oil until the desired moisture is attained. Place the pork on a rack inside a roasting pan. Press the crumbs on the top, ends, and down the sides. Cook until the pork is nearly pink in the center (145–150°F) about 1 hour 10 minutes. Let the pork rest for 10 minutes before adding the water to the pan. Reduce to a dark sauce and serve with the pork.

THE AUDUBON INN

Our sixteen elegantly appointed rooms offer comfort and romance. Each room includes private double whirlpool baths, custom-made queen-size four-poster beds, Scottish Lace curtains, and sitting area. Suites include DVD and 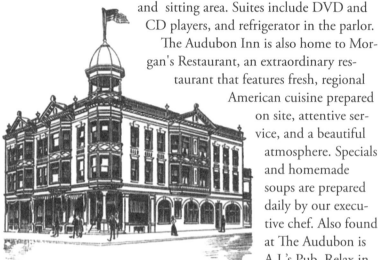 CD players, and refrigerator in the parlor. The Audubon Inn is also home to Morgan's Restaurant, an extraordinary restaurant that features fresh, regional American cuisine prepared on site, attentive service, and a beautiful atmosphere. Specials and homemade soups are prepared daily by our executive chef. Also found at The Audubon is A.J.'s Pub. Relax in the laid-back atmosphere and enjoy great food and fantastic drinks.

All of our guests enjoy a complimentary continental-plus breakfast, which consists of bagels, muffins, coffee cakes, hot and cold cereal, yogurt, and fresh fruits, as well as hot and cold beverages.

INNKEEPERS:	Michael & Stacy Shewey
ADDRESS:	45 N. Main St, Mayville, WI 53050
TELEPHONE:	(920) 387-5858
E-MAIL:	info@auduboninn.com
WEBSITE:	www.auduboninn.com
ROOMS:	16 Rooms
CHILDREN:	Welcome
PETS:	Pet-free environment

Grilled Pork Chops with Brown Ale & Mushroom Sauce

Makes 8 Servings

8 pork chops
1 shallot or ¼ medium onion
½ cup sliced mushrooms
1 clove garlic
1 tablespoon olive oil
2 cups demi-glace
1 cup brown ale
1 cup heavy cream

Heat your grill and cook pork chops 6–8 minutes per side, until the juices run clear. While the chops are grilling, dice the shallot or onion and heat a bit of olive oil in a saucepan over medium-high heat. Toss the shallot, mushroom, and garlic in the pan and sauté about 5 minutes, until the shallot is translucent. Add the brown ale, demi-glace, and heavy cream. Simmer 10 minutes until the sauce thickens. Pour the sauce over the chops and serve.

Tips and Variations

The internal temperature of a cooked pork chop should be around 160°F. Test the temperature by using a meat thermometer placed in the thickest part of the chop.

Duck Breasts with White Wine & Garlic Sauce

Makes 4 Servings

4 duck breasts
1 tablespoon olive oil
1 clove garlic
½ cup dry white wine
½ cup heavy cream
3 cups demi-glace
½ cup sliced mushrooms (optional)

Preheat oven to 375°F. Place the duck breasts skin-side-down in a large, heavy skillet and sear until the skin crisps. Remove to a baking dish and continue to cook in the oven until desired doneness.

Meanwhile, mince the garlic and sauté in olive oil with mushrooms if using. Cook until it just starts to brown. Add the white wine, cream, and demi-glace and simmer 10 minutes. Serve the duck breasts with the sauce.

Tips and Variations

If you score the fatty side of the breast before placing in the pan, this will help the fat to melt away. Make shallow, crosswise cuts in both directions (making a sort of grid). The internal temperature of a duck breast cooked to medium-rare is 130°F. Testing duck with a meat thermometer, however, will allow juices to escape. To test by touch, medium-rare duck should be firm with some give. Rare duck is softer to the touch.

Blackened Bleu Tenderloin

Makes 4 Servings

8 ounces butter

6 ounces bleu cheese

4 tenderloin steaks (8 ounces each)

4 slices bacon

4 tablespoons Cajun blackening seasoning

Preheat oven broiler. Soften the butter and mix with the bleu cheese. Roll in parchment paper to make a 1-inch log. Slice into ½-inch slices. Cut a pocket into the middle of each steak and lace one butter/bleu cheese slice inside. Wrap each steak in bacon and season with blackening seasoning. Sear each steak in a cast-iron pan over medium-high heat. Finish cooking in the oven until desired doneness is reached, about 4 minutes per side and then test for preference. Top each steak with a second slice of the butter and let rest long enough to melt before serving.

Blackening, as a cooking/spice method, was made popular by New Orleans chef Paul Prudhomme. The combination of butter, spices, and cooking method (using a very hot cast-iron skillet for cooking) creates a "black" crust and is a popular way of cooking both steak and fish.

NAESET-ROE INN

A romantic getaway, a spot to rest from your travels, a meeting place, or a businessperson's hideaway, all of these are the Naeset-Roe Inn. The inn is located within easy walking distance of great restaurants, art galleries and studios, live theater, pizza, a movie theater, and unique shopping.

Carl, your host and chef, has been preparing meals for almost 40 years and promises to excite your taste buds with something original

for breakfast. His philosophy is "Make it taste great, and let it have a little spark." Who says breakfast has to be bland and sweet? Your four-course breakfast promises to keep you going for anything you have planned for the day.

So come to historic Stoughton and experience a time gone by right here in the present. We're waiting for you.

INNKEEPER:	Carl Povlick
ADDRESS:	126 E Washington Street, Stoughton, WI 53589
TELEPHONE:	(608) 877-4150; (877) 787-5916
E-MAIL:	cpovlick@naesetroe.com
WEBSITE:	www.naesetroe.com
ROOMS:	4 Rooms
CHILDREN:	Facility inappropriate for children
PETS:	Resident pets only

Pecan Crusted Beef Tenderloin with Juniper Jus

Makes 10 Servings

2 well-trimmed, center cut beef tenderloins
 (not tied), 2–2½ pounds each
Salt and freshly ground pepper
4 tablespoons unsalted butter, divided
2 tablespoons extra-virgin olive oil
¼ cup ketchup
¼ cup Dijon mustard
4 large egg yolks
1 cup pecans, very finely chopped
3 shallots, thinly sliced
1 carrot, thinly sliced
1 tablespoon tomato paste
2 teaspoons dried juniper berries, crushed
1½ cups full-bodied red wine such as Syrah
1 cup beef demi-glace

Preheat oven to 425°F. Season the tenderloin all over with salt and pepper. In each of two large, deep skillets, melt 1 tablespoon butter and 1 tablespoon oil. Add the tenderloins to the skillets and cook over high heat until browned all over, about 8 minutes. Transfer to a rack and cool slightly. In a small bowl, combine the ketchup, mustard, and egg yolks and brush the mixture over the tenderloins. Transfer the meat to a large roasting pan and sprinkle with the pecans, pressing to help them adhere. Roast in the middle of the oven for about 25 minutes, until an instant-read thermometer inserted into the thickest part of each tenderloin registers 125°F (medium-rare). Transfer to a cutting board and let stand 10 minutes. Meanwhile, pour off the fat in one of the skillets used to brown the meat. Add the tomato paste and juniper berries and cook, stirring, for 2 minutes. Add the wine and cook over moderate heat, scraping up any browned bits, until the sauce is slightly thickened and reduced to ½ cup, about 10 minutes. Add the demi-glace and bring to a boil. Strain the sauce into a small saucepan using a fine sieve, pressing hard on the solids. Season the jus with salt and pepper and stir in the remaining 1 tablespoon butter. Carve the roast and serve with the juniper jus on the side.

Four Gables B&B

O ur 1906 Queen Anne historical home has survived straight-line winds, hail, snow, and torrents of rain. We purchased the home in 1982. Unfortunately, it was deteriorating after years of neglect, but we saw the potential in this gem and embarked on a painstaking restoration. In 1997 we opened the bed and breakfast

and began pampering our guests, a practice that continues today and ultimately brings them back for more. Our guests use two words to describe our home and our four-course breakfast: "romantic elegance."

Our back fields offer deer and wild turkey sightings on an almost daily basis and we are located within five miles of historic downtown La Crosse, the Mississippi and its sightseeing cruises. Other area attractions include local festivals, skiing, and historic sites.

INNKEEPERS:	Gerald & Nancy Jorgensen
ADDRESS:	W5648 US Highway 14-61, La Crosse, WI 54601
TELEPHONE:	(608) 788-7958
E-MAIL:	forgables@juno.com
WEBSITE:	www.wbba.org/inns/fourgablesbb_LaCrosse_WI.htm
ROOMS:	3 Rooms; Private & shared baths
CHILDREN:	Facility inappropriate for children
PETS:	Pet-free environment

Coq au Vin

Makes 6 Servings

"This is a quick gourmet recipe without all the fuss."
—INNKEEPER, *Four Gables B&B*

6 boneless skinless chicken breasts
Salt and pepper
1 tablespoon flour
¼ cup butter
Brandy
8 shallots, peeled
1¼ cups good white wine
½ pound morel mushrooms,
    or a combination of wild mushrooms
½ teaspoon Herbes de Provence
¼ cup heavy cream

Season the chicken pieces with salt and pepper; dust with flour. Melt the butter carefully in a large sauté pan or flameproof casserole, watch carefully so that is doesn't burn. Quickly brown the chicken on both sides. Remove from pan and keep warm. Pour a splash of brandy into the pot and set alight. When the flames have died down, add the shallots, wine, and mushrooms. Return the chicken to the pan and season with Herbes de Provence. Cover and simmer for approximately 30–35 minutes, or until done. Remove the chicken and arrange on a serving platter. Bring the juices to a rolling boil and allow to reduce just a bit. Lower the heat and add the cream, stirring to make a smooth sauce. Adjust the seasonings and pour the sauce over the chicken breasts to serve.

APPLE GROVE INN

Relax, unwind and enjoy the pristine beauty of the Apostle Islands National Lakeshore at our lovely country Bed & Breakfast, located just minutes from Bayfield, Wisconsin.

Take a stroll through our orchard and beautiful perennial gardens, watch the bluebirds feed in the morning sun, and be inspired

by the beauty of the Lake Superior countryside from our front porch.

As a Wisconsin certified Travel Green business, we are committed to preserving the environment, and are proud to let our guests know that we reuse, recycle, and buy local whenever possible.

INNKEEPERS:	Kathy & Greg Bergner
ADDRESS:	85095 State Highway 13, Bayfield, WI 54814
TELEPHONE:	(715) 779-9558; (888) 777-9558
E-MAIL:	Kathy@applegroveinn.net
WEBSITE:	www.applegroveinn.net
ROOMS:	4 Rooms
CHILDREN:	Facility inappropriate for children
PETS:	Resident pets only

Cranberry Chicken

Makes 6 Servings

*"This is one of my favorite recipes to make for special occasions.
It makes the house smell so good and looks beautiful on the plate.
I serve it with wild rice and it's a sensation for your taste buds. It was
adapted from a recipe found in the* Milwaukee Journal Sentinel.*"*

—INNKEEPER, *Apple Grove Inn*

½ cup plus 1 tablespoon flour, divided
1¼ teaspoons salt
3½ pounds chicken, skinless and boned
2–3 tablespoons butter
2–3 tablespoons cooking oil
¾ cup water
1 cup brown sugar
2 tablespoons red wine vinegar
½ teaspoon cinnamon
¼ teaspoon cloves
¼ teaspoon allspice
2 cups fresh or frozen cranberries

Preheat oven to 350°F. Combine ½ cup flour, 1 teaspoon salt,
and a dash of pepper. Roll the chicken pieces in the flour mixture,
then brown in oil and butter in a large skillet. When the chicken
has browned, remove from the pan and place in a baking dish.
Mix the water, brown sugar, vinegar, remaining flour, cinnamon,
cloves, allspice, and remaining salt in the skillet with the drippings.
Add the cranberries and cook slowly, stirring constantly, until the
cranberry skins pop and the mixture thickens (about 10 minutes).
Pour the sauce over the chicken and bake 30–40 minutes, or until
the chicken is tender.

KESSLER OLD WORLD GUESTHOUSE

WILLKOMMEN!! Come and experience a touch of the old world in the heart of Wisconsin.

This guesthouse was created and designed by Franz Kessler, and built by Franz and his wife, Kay, over a three-year period — along with a tremendous amount of help from family and friends. The design was inspired by German guesthouses that Franz and Kay have enjoyed, and uses many materials from Germany.

Experience a taste of the old world in one of the eight guestrooms, each themed after one of the old Germanic kingdoms. While many of these areas are not part of modern Germany (Alsace, Basel, Tyrol), they are part of the old German speaking kingdoms and reflect eight hundred years of family history.

The morning "frühstück" (traditional German breakfast) completes the experience.

INNKEEPERS:	Franz & Kay Kessler
ADDRESS:	1278 Alpine Court, Cleveland, WI 53015
TELEPHONE:	(920) 693-8379
E-MAIL:	kay@kesslerguesthouse.com
WEBSITE:	www.kesslerguesthouse.com
ROOMS:	8 Rooms
CHILDREN:	Inquire
PETS:	Pet-free environment

Sauerkraut & Buttons

Makes 6-8 Servings

"This recipe was passed down from my mother-in-law,
who was of German descent. Our children and grandchildren love it.
I sometimes double the recipe and still it all disappears."
—INNKEEPER, *Kessler Old World Guesthouse*

2 heaping cups flour
2 beaten eggs
Milk, approximately ½ cup
1 (14 ounce) package polska-kielbasa
1 package sauerkraut

In a medium bowl, combine the flour, eggs, and enough milk so that you have a workable dough. Roll sections of dough between your hands to make snake-like pieces. Bring 4-6 quarts of water to a boil. Cut 1-inch pieces from the rolled dough and drop into the boiling water. Boil 10 minutes, stirring occasionally, then drain. Slice the kielbasa into ¼-inch slices and brown. Drain and rinse the sauerkraut, reserving ½ cup of the juice. Add the sauerkraut, reserved juice, and dumplings to the kielbasa. Mix and enjoy!

The word Sauerkraut, translated, means sour cabbage. The cabbage is pickled over time and creates a great, sour complement to many dishes. Because salt is the main ingredient in the pickling process, rinsing the sauerkraut before using it is recommended.

CEDAR RIDGE B&B

Cedar Ridge is an historic family homestead dating back to the early 1800s, when Wisconsin was part of the Northwest Territory and Portage was the home of Fort Winnebago, a remote military frontier outpost. Today, the inn is surrounded by rugged natural beauty and rich local history. Come, enjoy the solitude of a country life from times past in a modern inn that features a 900-square-foot suite.

Less than two miles from Cedar Ridge you can dine and play golf at either the Portage Country Club or Saddle Ridge Golf Course. Want more? Five minutes in just about any direction will bring you to fishing, boating, canoeing, swimming, and picnic areas. Check out the nearby Amish community and enjoy quaint country stores, or walk the National Scenic Ice Age Trail. Also located nearby are the Ho-Chuck Casino, the Portage Center for the Arts, and the Crystal Grand Music Theatre.

INNKEEPER: Helen Rawson

ADDRESS: W6336 Highway 33 East, Portage, WI 53901

TELEPHONE: (608) 429-9254

E-MAIL: cedarridgebb@yahoo.com

WEBSITE: www.cedarridgebb.com

ROOMS: 1 Room

CHILDREN: Welcome

PETS: Pet-free environment

Sausage Stuffed Squash

Makes 2 Servings

1 medium acorn squash, 1–1½ pounds
1 Italian sausage link, casing removed
1 small onion, chopped
⅓ cup chopped green bell pepper
1 garlic clove, minced
1 medium tomato, chopped
¾ teaspoon Italian seasoning
⅛ teaspoon salt
⅛ teaspoon pepper
¼ cup shredded Parmesan cheese

Cut the squash in half lengthwise and discard the seeds. Place cut-side-down in a microwave-safe 11x7-inch baking dish. Cover and microwave on high for 10–12 minutes, or until tender. Meanwhile, crumble the sausage into a large skillet. Add the onion, green pepper, and garlic and cook over medium heat until the meat is no longer pink. Drain and then stir in the tomato, Italian seasoning, salt, and pepper. Turn the squash cut-side-up and stuff with the sausage mixture. Sprinkle with Parmesan cheese, cover, and microwave on high 2–3 minutes, or until heated through.

Fabulous Fast Shrimp

Makes 4 Servings

"This is delicious."

—INNKEEPER, *Cedar Ridge B&B*

1 tablespoon butter or margarine
2 stalks celery, chopped
¼ cup sliced green onions
¼ cup chopped green bell pepper
1 pound fresh large shrimp, shelled and deveined
1 (10¾ ounce) can cream of shrimp soup
½ cup water
Generous dash of ground red pepper
Hot cooked rice
Paprika

Heat the butter in a skillet over medium-high heat. Add the celery, green onion, and bell peppers to the pan and cook until tender. Add the shrimp and cook 3–5 minutes, until the shrimp are pink. Add the soup, water, and red pepper to the pan and heat through. Serve over rice and sprinkle with paprika.

Tips and Variations

Because fresh shrimp should be used within 24 hours of purchase, frozen shrimp can be used as an alternative. For best results, purchase frozen shrimp with the shells still intact. Frozen, shelled, and deveined shrimp lose some of their flavor. To defrost, place in the refrigerator or cold water. Do not heat, as this will begin the cooking process.

Peppery Pepper Fajitas

Makes 4-6 Servings

*"Cheese isn't traditional with fajitas and these don't even
really need it, but a bit of shredded Chihuahua cheese melted
on top of the veggies is a very tasty addition to this dish."*

—INNKEEPER, *Cedar Ridge B&B*

Juice from 2 limes
2 tablespoons corn oil
2 teaspoons coarse ground pepper
1 teaspoon cumin
1 jalapeno pepper, chopped
2 tablespoons fresh cilantro
1 teaspoon Mexican oregano
2 red bell peppers
2 orange bell peppers
4 large Portobello mushrooms
8 soft-shelled tortillas

SALSA
4 medium red ripe tomatoes
1 small red onion
2 fresh jalapenos
2 tablespoons fresh cilantro
½ teaspoon salt
Juice of 1 lime
¼ teaspoon coarse pepper
¼ teaspoon ground cumin

Prepare a marinade by combining lime juice, corn oil, pepper,
cumin, jalapeno, cilantro, and oregano. Slice the bell peppers and
mushrooms into long bite-sized slices and add to the marinade.
Toss to coat, cover, and set aside.

Prepare the salsa by chopping tomato, onion, jalapeno, and cilantro and combining with salt, lime juice, pepper, and cumin. Toss
to combine and set aside.

Preheat oven to 350°F. Cover the tortilla shells to keep them
from drying out and place them in the oven to warm. Heat a
large, heavy-bottomed pan. When the pan is very hot, remove
about ¼–⅓ of the vegetables from the marinade and cook, stirring, for 3–4 minutes, until crisp tender. Remove to a plate and
repeat until all the vegetables are cooked. Serve with warmed
tortillas and salsa.

INN ON MAIN STREET

Centrally located in Stevens Point, Wisconsin, The Inn on Main Street, LLC, resides across the street from "Old Main," the University of Wisconsin — Stevens Point's original building. Surrounded by tall stately trees, this lannon stone colonial revival house was built in 1922 for the second President of the then Normal School.

Stevens Point is privileged to have a 30-mile biking/hiking route, "The Green Circle Trail." The Wisconsin River, located a mile from the b&b, serves as the main playground for our resident fishing guide, and Sentry World Golf is one of the finest courses in Central Wisconsin.

Our guests are most important to us and providing a restful experience is our main goal.

INNKEEPERS:	Kathy & Ron Schwarz
ADDRESS:	2141 Main Street, Stevens Point, WI 54481
TELEPHONE:	(715) 343-0373
E-MAIL:	kathysinn@charter.net
WEBSITE:	www.innonmainstreet.com
ROOMS:	3 Rooms; Private & shared baths
CHILDREN:	Inquire
PETS:	Pet-free environment

Spaghetti Bake

Makes 8 Servings

*"This recipe is very good when serving a hungry crowd.
Everyone seems to love it and are able to make little additions
to their liking, such as green peppers and/or mushrooms."*
—INNKEEPER, *The Inn on Main Street*

2 pounds ground hamburger or
    Italian sausages removed from their casings
2 (8 ounce) cans tomato sauce
3 cups water
2 packages spaghetti sauce mix
Oregano, basil, and pepper to taste
1 (1 pound) package spaghetti noodles,
    broken up
¼ cup margarine
5 tablespoons flour
1 teaspoon salt
2 cups milk
¼ cup shredded cheese
    (Cheddar, Jack or mozzarella)
¼ cup Parmesan cheese

Preheat oven to 350°F. Brown the hamburger or sausage in a deep skillet and then drain. Add the tomato sauce, water, spaghetti sauce mix, and seasonings. Simmer 30 minutes. Cook the spaghetti and drain. Melt the butter in a saucepan. Stir in the flour and salt and add the milk slowly. Stir until thick. Add the cheeses and stir until melted. In a 13x9-inch pan, layer in the following order: half of the spaghetti, half of the sauce, half of the cheese. Repeat and top with additional Parmesan cheese. Bake 15–20 minutes. Serve with garlic bread.

Phipps Inn

W e're close to home, yet a hundred years away. Let the Phipps Inn become your favorite escape!

The Phipps Inn is the premier Queen Anne Victorian bed and breakfast in Wisconsin's St. Croix River Valley. It is located on Historic Third Street in the beautiful city of Hudson, a short walk from downtown restaurants, shops, and the river.

We offer many common areas including three parlors, two porches, and a billiards room. We are known for our four-course gourmet breakfasts and our friendly yet unobtrusive hospitality. All Phipps Inn guest rooms have fireplaces, whirlpool tubs, and private baths. We specialize in the three Rs: romance, relax, and refresh.

INNKEEPERS:	Mary Ellen & Rich Cox
ADDRESS:	1005 3rd Street, Hudson, WI 54016
TELEPHONE:	(715) 386-0800
E-MAIL:	info@phippsinn.com
WEBSITE:	www.phippsinn.com
ROOMS:	6 Rooms
CHILDREN:	Inquire
PETS:	Pet-free environment

Greek Spaghetti

Makes 4–6 Servings

"This is a great way to serve leftover ham or turkey after the holidays."
—INNKEEPER, *Phipps Inn*

½ pound fettuccini noodles
1 (10 ounce) package frozen chopped spinach,
    thawed and drained
¼ cup minced onion
2 cloves minced garlic
¼ of a large green bell pepper, chopped
1½ cups chopped celery
1 small jar pimentos (4 ounces)
1 (10¾ ounce) can cream of chicken soup
½ cup mayonnaise
½ cup sour cream
½ pound Monterey Jack cheese, shredded
1 pound chopped ham or turkey
Bread crumbs
Parmesan cheese

Preheat oven to 350°F. Cook the noodles and drain. Mix together all of the ingredients except the bread crumbs and Parmesan and place in a 2-quart casserole. Sprinkle the bread crumbs and Parmesan over the top and bake 45–60 minutes.

You can also make this as layered casserole. Mix together onion, garlic, bell pepper, celery, pimentos, soup, mayo, and sour cream. Layer the dish as follows: noodles, spinach, veggie/soup mixture, meat, Monterey Jack, Parmesan, and finally bread crumbs.

A VICTORIAN SWAN ON WATER

"Last night we were two weary travelers and today we are surrounded by elegance, rested, pampered, and delighted in your warm companionship. Thanks for your most memorable hospitality." —GUEST

A Victorian gem of a bed and breakfast welcomes you to Central Wisconsin where green means hiking and biking on the beautiful Green Circle Trail, or kayaking down the Plover or Wisconsin Rivers. Stroll our historic Main Street or walk along the Wisconsin River. Come back to a whirlpool, sauna, or massage, or just sit in front of a fireplace and read.

Our mission since 1986 has always been to provide our guests with a setting that is clean, comfortable, and beautiful, a setting with good food and great conversation.

INNKEEPER:	Joan Ouellette
ADDRESS:	1716 Water Street, Stevens Point, WI 54481
TELEPHONE:	(715) 345-0595; (800) 454-9886
E-MAIL:	victorianswan@charter.net
WEBSITE:	www.victorianswan.com
ROOMS:	4 Rooms
CHILDREN:	Children age 3 and older welcome
PETS:	Pet-free environment

Basic Egg Foo Yung

Makes 5 Servings

"This dish is a wonderful vehicle for using leftovers. I took a Chinese cooking class in the 1980s and Egg Foo Yung became one of our favorite supper dishes. I found that besides being easy, adding different vegetables, meats, or gravy could add variety to our mealtime."

—INNKEEPER, *A Victorian Swan on Water*

¼ cup diced or sliced green onions
½ cup fresh bean sprouts
¼ cup cooked meat
  (shrimp, beef, chicken, or pork)
½ teaspoon soy sauce
Salt and pepper, to taste
2 extra large eggs
Canola cooking oil

BROWN SAUCE
1 cup chicken broth
1 tablespoon cornstarch
2 tablespoons water
¼ teaspoon salt
Pepper, to taste
2 teaspoons soy sauce
1 teaspoon sherry or vermouth
½ teaspoon sugar
¼ teaspoon sesame oil (optional)

Before you begin, make sure that all of your vegetables are drained and dry. Combine all of the ingredients, except the eggs and oil, together in a bowl. Stir in the eggs but do not beat. Heat about ½-inch of oil in a fry pan or wok. Pour about ¼ cup of the mixture into the hot oil and let cook until slightly brown. Turn the egg patty over and cook for about 2 minutes longer. Remove from the pan and keep warm until all the patties are made. Serve hot over rice with brown sauce or gravy.

For the sauce: Simmer the chicken broth in a small kettle. Mix together the water and cornstarch. Combine the remaining ingredients and add, with cornstarch mixture, to the broth. Stir until it bubbles and is clear.

Fruit Specialties, Desserts, Bars, & Cookies

Fruit Specialties, Desserts, Bars, & Cookies

We think you'll like this quote
as much as we do and it goes like this:
"Life is short. Eat dessert first."

DOOR COUNTY
LIGHTHOUSE INN

Travel to beautiful Door County and experience our rich maritime history while visiting the ten lighthouses that dot the 300 miles of shoreline. Our B&B makes you feel like you are staying in the eleventh lighthouse of Door County.

Delight in the warm homey atmosphere filled with lighthouse décor. Start each day's adventure with a full breakfast and great conversation with fellow lighthouse and Door County enthusiasts.

Winter in Door County includes sleigh rides, wineries, fireside lunch, the Door County Progressive Dinner, and our Romance Packages. In summer and fall we offer packages such as the Self

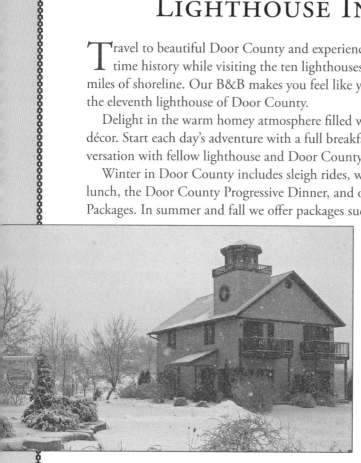

Guided Lighthouse Tour, Trolley Lighthouse Package, Trolley Ghost Adventures, and a day trip to Rock Island's Pottawatomie Lighthouse.

INNKEEPERS:	Claire & Frank Murphy
ADDRESS:	4639 Orchard Road, Egg Harbor, WI 54209
TELEPHONE:	(920) 868-9088; (866) 868-9088
E-MAIL:	info@dclighthouseinn.com
WEBSITE:	www.dclighthouseinn.com
ROOMS:	5 Rooms
CHILDREN:	Inquire
PETS:	Pet-free environment

First Assistant Citrus Fruit Cup

Makes 6 Servings

"This recipe was adapted from the
Williams Sonoma Kitchen Library."

—INNKEEPER, *Door County Lighthouse Inn*

1$\frac{1}{3}$ cups water
$\frac{2}{3}$ cup sugar
1 vanilla bean, split in half lengthwise
4 large naval oranges
2 large grapefruits
Fresh mint sprigs

Combine the water, sugar, and vanilla bean together in a sauce-pan over medium-high heat. Cook, stirring constantly, to make a syrup. Peel and segment the oranges and grapefruits and place the citrus pieces in a serving bowl. Take the saucepan off the heat and remove the vanilla bean. Pour the syrup over the citrus pieces and toss to coat. Garnish with mint sprigs and serve.

Tips and Variations

For an extra treat, serve this citrus cup with a scoop of vanilla ice cream on the side. Also, because fresh fruit tastes best when it is in season, try substituting other citruses throughout the year. Tangerines, tangelos, and clementines (small mandarin oranges) are just a few alternatives to oranges. Grapefruit is available year-round because it is grown in so many different regions.

WHITE SHUTTERS

Enjoy a "king of the hill" view of the countryside from this 1890 farmhouse. The Spring Valley and Golden Corners rooms are named for two of the nearby country roads. Spring Valley is furnished with a queen and twin bed, and a 1906 family heirloom fainting couch accents the room. Golden Corners is furnished with a double bed and features vintage family photographs along the walls; braided rugs complement the antique décor. The Guest Nest, a cozy sitting room, provides a perfect place to read and relax and

the restored 1900 granary on the property includes an indoor sitting area and a porch that beckons guests to sit and enjoy the peaceful setting.

White Shutters is located midway between Horicon Marsh and the Northern Kettle Moraine State Forest. Nearby attractions include Widmer's Cheese Cellars, the Ice Age Trail, the EAA Air Venture Museum, General Store Antique Mall, Lake Winnebago, The Golf Club at Camelot, and Sunburst Ski Area.

INNKEEPERS:	Rollie Glass & Lorna Schwingle-Glass
ADDRESS:	W265 County Road H, Lomira, WI 53048
TELEPHONE:	(920) 269-4056
E-MAIL:	whiteshutters@nconnect.net
WEBSITE:	www.thewhiteshutters.com
ROOMS:	2 Rooms; Private & shared baths
CHILDREN:	Inquire
PETS:	Resident pets only

Peaches & Cream

Makes 9 Servings

"My sister-in-law made this dessert for a family gathering and it was a hit! We often serve it as a baked treat to our b&b guests."

INNKEEPER, *White Shutters*

¾ cup flour
1 (four-serving) package vanilla pudding mix,
    not instant
1 teaspoon baking powder
1 beaten egg
½ cup milk
3 tablespoons butter, melted
1 (16 ounce) can peaches
8 ounces cream cheese
½ cup plus 1 tablespoon sugar, divided
½ teaspoon cinnamon

Preheat oven to 350°F. In a medium bowl, stir together the flour, pudding mix, and baking powder. In a separate bowl, combine the egg, milk, and melted butter. Add the wet mixture to the dry ingredients and mix well. Spread the batter in a buttered 8-inch square baking dish. Drain the peaches, reserving ⅓ cup juice. Chop the peaches and sprinkle over the batter. Beat together the cream cheese, ½ cup sugar, and reserved peach liquid and pour over the peaches. Combine the remaining tablespoon sugar with the cinnamon and sprinkle over the top. Bake 45 minutes.

VICTORIA ON MAIN B&B

It has been our pleasure to welcome guests to the Victoria on Main Bed and Breakfast for over 19 years. We are located in the historic district near downtown Whitewater, and across the street from the University of Wisconsin–Whitewater. Our Queen Anne revival home, built in 1895, features different woods in each room. The bedrooms are decorated with wallpapers, lace curtains, and antiques. The comfortable historic beds are covered with antique linens and lace trimmings, and down comforters and pillows. As a Shaklee distributor, we use all Earth friendly products.

Everyone loves our small town and everything it has to offer. Hiking in the Kettle Moraine State Forest, swimming or boating at

Whitewater Lake, attending plays at Young Auditorium or the Fireside, and eating at one of our many restaurants are just a few of the things to do. Check us out!

INNKEEPER: Nancy Wendt
ADDRESS: 622 W Main Street, Whitewater, WI 53190
TELEPHONE: (262) 473-8400
E-MAIL: viconmain@sbcglobal.net
WEBSITE: www.wbba.org/inns/victoriaonmainbb_whitewater.html
ROOMS: 3 Rooms; Private & shared baths
CHILDREN: Facility inappropriate for children
PETS: Resident pets only

Cherry Berries in the Snow

Plan ahead, this dish needs to be refrigerated overnight.

Makes 15 Servings

"Everyone loves this dish. It's a must for Christmas."

—INNKEEPER, *Victoria on Main B&B*

6 egg whites
½ teaspoon cream of tartar
1¾ cups sugar, separated
1 teaspoon vinegar
2 teaspoons vanilla extract
8 ounces cream cheese
2 cups whipping cream, whipped
2 cups miniature marshmallows
1 (21 ounce) can cherry pie filling
1 (16 ounce) package frozen strawberries, thawed

Preheat oven to 300°F. In a medium bowl, beat the egg whites until stiff. Slowly add cream of tartar, 1½ cups sugar, vinegar, and 1 teaspoon vanilla. Pour the mixture into a greased 9x13-inch baking dish. Bake 30 minutes before reducing oven temperature to 200°F and baking an additional 30 minutes. Cool. In a medium bowl, mix together the cream cheese, remaining sugar, and 1 teaspoon vanilla. Fold in the whipped cream and marshmallows and pour over the cooled meringue. Refrigerate 12 hours or overnight before serving. Combine the cherries and strawberries and pour over the meringue when serving.

LAZY CLOUD

Relax at the Lazy Cloud in the beautiful Lake Geneva, Wisconsin area. All of our accommodations are done in our signature romantic style: Each accommodation has a luxurious double whirlpool tub and a blazing fireplace, and each one is decorated in an individual theme with a daybed, couch, or loveseat for lounging, and a small dining area for two. Additionally, they all have candles, fluffy bathrobes, bubble bath, and bath pillows for your use. The game Enchanted Evening (a romantic couple's game) is also in each

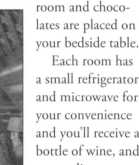

room and chocolates are placed on your bedside table.

Each room has a small refrigerator and microwave for your convenience and you'll receive a bottle of wine, and a complimentary basket with microwave popcorn and flavored gourmet hot chocolate and cappuccino. We also provide a radio with cassette and CD player so you may relax and enjoy your favorite music.

INNKEEPERS:	Keith & Carol Tiffany
ADDRESS:	Lake Geneva, WI 53147
TELEPHONE:	(262) 275-3322
E-MAIL:	love@lazycloud.com
WEBSITE:	www.lazycloud.com
ROOMS:	10 Rooms
CHILDREN:	Facility inappropriate for children
PETS:	Pet-free environment

Apple Crisp

Makes 9 Servings

"This is always a hit for the guests,
especially in the cold winter months."
—INNKEEPER, *Lazy Cloud*

5–6 apples, peeled and sliced
2 teaspoons cinnamon
½ cup soft butter
¾ cup flour
1 cup brown sugar

Preheat oven to 350°F. Place the apples in a 9x9-inch pan or deep-dish pie plate. Sprinkle cinnamon over the apples. In a small bowl, mix together the butter, flour, and sugar, being careful not to over mix. Crumble the mixture over the apples and bake 45 minutes.

Tips and Variations

For a shortcut, you may use peeled, sliced frozen apples. Put the apples in the pan the night before and let them thaw in the refrigerator overnight. Drain before topping.

WESTBY HOUSE VICTORIAN INN

Return to a simpler time, to a b&b that combines the right levels of history, comfort, and hospitality. The Westby House Inn is truly a Victorian Grand Lady that is steeped with period details, vernacular architecture, stained-glass windows, antique accents, and

elegant interior woodwork and turrets. The wrap-around porch and outdoor deck are perfect havens for an evening of conversation and watching the world go by in this quaint Norwegian community.

The Westby House property's banquet and dining facilities are available for small and intimate weddings, dinner parties, and special occasion celebrations. The Lunch and Tearoom are open April through October for lunch and events. Westby House is the perfect retreat for celebrating an anniversary or birthday, special celebration, or a girlfriend's getaway.

INNKEEPERS:	Marie & Mike Cimino
ADDRESS:	200 West State Street, Westby, WI 54667
TELEPHONE:	(608) 634-4112; (800) 434-7439
E-MAIL:	info@westbyhouse.com
WEBSITE:	www.westbyhouse.com
ROOMS:	5 Rooms; 4 Cottage suites
CHILDREN:	Children age 10 and older welcome
PETS:	Pet-Free Environment

Pumpkin Walnut Crisp

Makes 8 Servings

*"This recipe is a great way to start off breakfast in the fall season!
It can be baked ahead and cooled. Heat through before serving."*

—INNKEEPER, *Westby House Victorian Inn*

2 (15 ounce) cans pumpkin

1 cup sugar

¾ cup evaporated milk

3 large eggs

1 teaspoon cinnamon

1 teaspoon nutmeg

1 teaspoon vanilla extract

WALNUT CRISP TOPPING

¾ cup firmly packed brown sugar

¾ cup quick-cooking oats

¾ cup coarsely chopped walnuts

2 tablespoons all-purpose flour

¼ teaspoon cinnamon

6 tablespoons butter, melted

Preheat oven to 350°F and lightly grease an 8-inch square baking dish or 8 small ramekins. In a large bowl, whisk together the pumpkin, sugar, milk, eggs, cinnamon, nutmeg, and vanilla. Pour the mixture into the prepared dish. In a medium bowl, combine the brown sugar, oats, walnuts, flour, and cinnamon for the walnut crisp topping. Add the melted butter to the topping mixture and stir until combined. Sprinkle the walnut topping over the pumpkin mixture and bake 45–50 minutes, or until center is set. Serve warm with whipped cream and cinnamon.

Spring Fruit Salad

Makes 6–8 Servings

⅓ cup fresh lemon juice
3 tablespoons apricot jam
¼ cup brown sugar
2 tangerines, peeled, sectioned,
    and seeds removed
2 naval oranges, peeled
    and sectioned
1 banana, peeled and sliced
1 firm pear, cored and sliced
1 cup Ribier grapes
1 cup Thompson seedless grapes
1 cup dried cranberries
    or pitted cherries
Plain yogurt
Granola

In a large bowl, mix together the lemon juice, jam, and brown sugar. Stir until well blended. Add the fruits and mix well. Let the fruit marinate for at least one hour before serving.

To serve: Spoon the fruit salad into parfait glasses and top with yogurt and granola.

Hot Apple Pie Dip

Makes 2 Cups

"This recipe was adapted from the
Nabisco Appetizers & More *magazine."*
—INNKEEPER, *Westby House Victorian Inn*

8 ounces cream cheese
2 tablespoons brown sugar
½ teaspoon cinnamon
¼ teaspoon nutmeg
¼ teaspoon allspice
1 apple, chopped and divided
¾ cup reduced fat shredded Cheddar cheese
1 tablespoon finely chopped pecans

Preheat oven to 375°F. In a medium bowl, mix together the cream cheese, sugar, and spices until well blended. Stir in half of the chopped apple. Spread the mixture into an 8-inch pie plate or small casserole dish. Top with the remaining apples, Cheddar cheese, and pecans and bake 10–12 minutes, or until heated through. Serve with crackers.

Tips and Variations

Try making your own sweet dessert chips to go along with this dip. Brush flour tortillas with butter, cut into wedges, and sprinkle with a cinnamon/sugar mixture. Bake at 350°F until golden brown. Wheat thins, butter crackers, and apple chips are great as well.

THE LAMP POST INN

Welcome to our 1874 Victorian home packed with antiques and adventure. You can soak in the claw foot tub filled with bubbles or relax in our over-sized Jacuzzi. Feel free to dress up in our antique clothes and jewelry for pictures or a night out on the town. There are antique victrolas in all of the rooms and hundreds

of board games to play.

We are located just six blocks from the famous Fireside Dinner Theatre and four blocks from the newly developed river walk and bike trail. People from Chicago come to shop in our historic downtown shops such as I Love Funky's, Soap n Pepper, and Ravenwood. Whether you are a first time b&b-er or a seasoned one, you'll find our inn intriguing and cozy. Many of our guests return every year to reminisce and enjoy "the best breakfast they ever had."

INNKEEPERS:	Debbie & Mike Rusch
ADDRESS:	408 South Main Street, Fort Atkinson, WI 53538
TELEPHONE:	(920) 563-6561
E-MAIL:	lamppostinn@compufort.com
WEBSITE:	www.thelamppostinn.com
ROOMS:	3 Rooms
CHILDREN:	Inquire
PETS:	Pet-free environment

Perfect Raspberry Pie

Makes 1 Pie

"The people I cook for said they didn't want the recipe for this pie,
they just wanted me to bake them more!"
—INNKEEPER, *The Lamp Post Inn*

1 10-inch baked pie crust
4 cups fresh raspberries, divided
1 cup water, divided
3 tablespoons cornstarch
1 cup sugar

Place 3 cups of the raspberries in the baked pie shell. Mix ⅔ cup of water with the remaining 1 cup of raspberries in a saucepan and cook over medium-high heat for 3 minutes; set aside. In a small bowl, combine the remaining ⅓ cup water with the cornstarch and sugar. Add the sugar mixture to the cooked raspberry mixture and simmer together until clear. Cool and then pour over the fresh berries in the pie shell. Serve with whipped cream.

Did you know that raspberries are high in fiber, vitamins A and C, calcium, and a cancer-preventing substance called ellagic acid? This super fruit is traditionally harvested in summer and fall. Some raspberry tips: Don't wash your berries until you are ready to use them, refrigerate immediately after purchasing, and eat within 1-2 days. Frozen raspberries will keep best in vacuum-sealed packages.

THE SAWYER HOUSE B&B

The Sawyer House B&B was initially built in 1902 by Dr. Albert Kreizer. The home is a Late Queen Anne Victorian that was renovated in 1999 and transformed into a bed and breakfast. This turn-of-the-century house is located in a quiet neighborhood in Sturgeon Bay, but is still close to all of the Door County attractions.

Experience warm hospitality with sweets in the evening and a homemade breakfast in the morning. All dishes have nutritional information available upon request and special dietary needs are not a problem to accommodate.

"We have enjoyed our stay here. It was so relaxing and peaceful to be here. The hospitality is outstanding and the breakfast was wonderful. We love your home!"

—Guest

INNKEEPER:	Ruth Norton
ADDRESS:	101 S Lansing Avenue, Sturgeon Bay, WI 54235
TELEPHONE:	(920) 746-1640; (888) 746-1614
E-MAIL:	sawyerhouse@itol.com
WEBSITE:	www.bbonline.com/wi/sawyer
ROOMS:	5 Rooms
CHILDREN:	Facility inappropriate for children
PETS:	Pet-free environment

Rhubarb Pie

Makes 1 Pie

*"This was my mother's recipe and it brings back memories
for me each time I make it. Even guests who think
they don't like rhubarb pie love this one."*
—INNKEEPER, *The Sawyer House B&B*

1 9-inch pie crust
3 cups rhubarb, diced
2 whole eggs
2 tablespoons milk
1½ cups sugar
3 tablespoons flour
¼ teaspoon salt
¼ teaspoon nutmeg

TOPPING
¼ cup margarine
¼ cup brown sugar
½ cup flour

Preheat oven to 400°F. Place the diced rhubarb in the pie crust.
In a medium bowl, mix together the eggs, milk, sugar, flour, salt,
and nutmeg and pour over the rhubarb. Crumble together the
margarine, brown sugar, and flour for the topping and sprinkle
over the top of the pie. Bake 1 hour.

BREWERY CREEK B&B INN AND BREWPUB

The Brewery Creek Brewpub Restaurant (yes, we brew beer too!) has been serving lunch and dinner to inn guests and the general public since 1998. The restaurant is a small and intimate space that seats about 40 and is located in the same building as the main inn.

We believe that to make really good food you need to slow down, get involved, and follow two basic principles. First, use quality

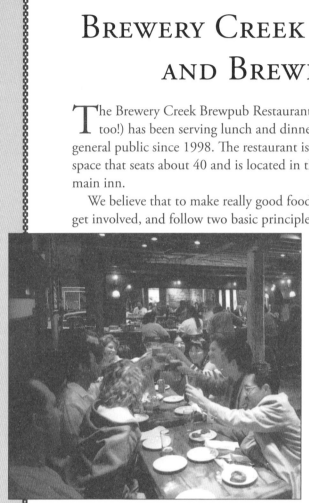

ingredients; there is no substitute and they are a cook's best friends. Use them whenever you can. Second, make your food from scratch, from basic ingredients. We do. So, if you are staying with us, or even if you're just in town for a few hours, stop by for a beer, a burger, a sandwich, steak, pasta, or an entrée salad. And save room for a great dessert.

INNKEEPERS:	Deb & Jeff Donaghue
ADDRESS:	23 Commerce Street, Mineral Point, WI 53565
TELEPHONE:	(608) 987-3298
E-MAIL:	info@brewerycreek.com
WEBSITE:	www.brewerycreek.com
ROOMS:	5 Rooms; 2 Cottages
CHILDREN:	Children age 12 and older welcome
PETS:	Resident pets only

Kentucky Bourbon Pecan Pie

Makes 1 Pie

*"This is a fairly traditional, restaurant-style
pecan pie that we have adapted."*
—INNKEEPER, *Brewery Creek B&B Inn and Brewpub*

1 unbaked pie shell
1¼ cups dark corn syrup
1 cup dark brown sugar
4 tablespoons butter
1 cup pecans, halves or pieces
4 eggs
1 teaspoon vanilla extract
2 tablespoons straight bourbon whiskey
2 tablespoons heavy cream

Preheat oven to 350°F and line a 9-inch pie dish with the unbaked crust. Melt the corn syrup and brown sugar together in a
saucepan over medium-high heat. Stir frequently to prevent sticking and burning. When the mixture begins to boil, add the butter
and nuts and remove from heat. In a medium bowl, beat the eggs
until they are just mixed. Add the vanilla, whiskey, and cream
to the sugar mixture and then temper the eggs — whisk a small
amount of the hot sugar mixture into the eggs in order to heat
them and prevent them from scrambling. Add the egg mixture to
the sugar mixture, whisking to combine. Pour the mixture into
the pie shell and place the pie plate on a cookie sheet to catch any
batter that may boil over. Bake 45–60 minutes.

Tips and Variations

Substitute either brandy or rum for the whiskey. You can also use
light brown sugar and light corn syrup, but the flavor is not as deep.

Sunnyfield Farm B&B

*S*tarscapes*, the original three-dimensional ceiling mural of the nighttime sky, with hundreds of glow-in-the dark stars including the Milk Way Galaxy and shooting stars, allows guests to stargaze in luxurious comfort from their queen-sized bed. This unique third-floor studio offers accommodations for a romantic retreat, a writer's paradise, or a traveler's home away from home.

Each morning, guests will feast upon a healthy country breakfast prepared by your hostess and served in our light and spacious dining room. Fuel up before you head out for a day of exploring some of Wisconsin's most popular tourist attractions, whether it's the Volk Field Military Museum, the Omaha Bike Trail, Castle Rock Lake, the Castle Rock Golf Course, Necedah Wildlife Refuge, or the many interesting sites in local Amish communities.

INNKEEPER: Susanne Soltvedt
ADDRESS: N6692 Batko Road, Camp Douglas, WI 54618
TELEPHONE: (608) 427-3686; (888) 839-0232
E-MAIL: soltvedt@mwt.net
WEBSITE: www.sunnyfield.net
ROOMS: 4 Rooms; Private & shared baths
CHILDREN: Welcome
PETS: Welcome

Jewels Under Cake Dessert

Makes 15 Servings

*"Guests have asked me to serve only this at breakfast
so that they can eat more of it. I have made boxes to go
for hiking and biking and I often halve the recipe
for smaller groups. The original recipe was a 1991 winner at the
Warrens Cranfest Cook-off. I found it in a church cookbook."*
—INNKEEPER, *Sunnyfield Farm B&B*

20 ounces crushed pineapple

6 cups cranberries, fresh or frozen

3½ cups sugar

3½ tablespoons cornstarch

1 tablespoon vanilla extract

¾ teaspoon salt

1 box yellow cake mix

1 cup melted butter

1 cup chopped nuts

1 cup coconut

Preheat oven to 325°F. Slightly drain the crushed pineapple;
set aside. Mix the cranberries, sugar, and cornstarch together in
saucepan over low heat. Cook until the berries are tender being
careful not to burn them. When the mixture is thick, add the
vanilla and salt. Pour the mixture into a 9x13-inch baking dish
and allow to cool. Pour the drained pineapple over the cooled
cranberries. Sprinkle the cake mix over the top and drizzle with
butter. Top with nuts and coconut and bake 1 hour. Serve warm
or cold.

ALBANY HOUSE

A warmly inviting country house from the turn-of-the-century, Albany House has been welcoming travelers for over 20 years. Three acres of grounds and gardens, art, antiques, and a distinctive decorating style make Albany House a perennial favorite of the discerning traveler. Hearty homemade breakfasts, a highlight of any stay, emphasize comfort food with a twist. Dishes feature fresh, seasonal produce and local products are used whenever possible. Regional artisan cheeses are often sampled with breakfast.

Burn up any extra calories on the two area bicycle trails or canoe the nearby river. For those who prefer a kinder, gentler activity before heading out for a day of exploration, there are hammocks and front porch swings.

INNKEEPERS: Ken & Margie Stoup
ADDRESS: 405 South Mill Street, Albany, WI 53502
TELEPHONE: (608) 862-3636; (866) 977-7000
E-MAIL: innkeeper@albanyhouse.com
WEBSITE: www.albanyhouse.com
ROOMS: 6 Rooms; Private & shared baths
CHILDREN: Children age 10 and older welcome
PETS: Pet-free environment

Pumpkin Bread Pudding

Makes 8 Servings

"My friend, Victoria, gave me this recipe.
I finally tried it four years later and have been making it
to rave reviews ever since.
It's very light and we serve it at breakfast."

—INNKEEPER, *Albany House*

1 (8 ounce) baguette,
sliced ½-inch thick
4 large eggs
1 quart half & half
1 (15 ounce) can pumpkin purée
1 cup packed brown sugar
1 tablespoon pumpkin pie spice
1 teaspoon vanilla extract
¼ teaspoon salt
Confectioners' sugar
Whipped Cream

Preheat oven to 300°F and butter an 8-inch square or 2-quart baking dish. Toast the bread slices on a baking sheet in the oven, turning occasionally until lightly browned, 20–25 minutes. In a large bowl, whisk together the eggs, half & half, pumpkin, brown sugar, spice, vanilla, and salt. Add the toasted bread and cover with plastic wrap, pressing directly onto the surface. Place a plate small enough to fit inside the bowl on top of the plastic. Weigh the plate down using a canned item. Let sit for 25 minutes.

Increase oven temperature to 350°F. Transfer the mixture to the buttered dish, spreading evenly. Place the baking dish on a sheet pan and bake 60–70 minutes, until a toothpick inserted in the center comes away clean. Serve warm or at room temperature, dusted with confectioners' sugar and topped with whipped cream.

Peach Pudding

Makes 4 Servings

*"This is a recipe that my mother made for many years.
I have been known to double or triple it as needed."*

—INNKEEPER, *Albany House*

3 tablespoons butter
1 cup sugar, divided
1 cup flour
½ teaspoon baking soda
1 teaspoon baking powder
⅛ teaspoon salt
1 cup buttermilk
2 cups sliced and peeled peaches
½ teaspoon nutmeg
½ teaspoon cinnamon
⅔ cup boiling water

Preheat oven to 350°F. In a large bowl, cream together the butter and ½ cup sugar. In a medium bowl, sift together the flour, baking salt, baking powder, and salt. Add the dry mixture to the butter mixture alternately with the buttermilk. Stir well and pour the mixture into a 1½-quart casserole dish. Combine the peaches, the remaining sugar, and the boiling water and pour over the mixture in the casserole. Do not stir. Bake 45 minutes.

Black Bottom Cupcakes

Makes 2 Dozen

*'My aunt always brought these to family picnics.
My sister has been making them ever since and
I got the recipe from her. They freeze well."*

—INNKEEPER, *Albany House*

1 (8 ounce) package cream cheese
1 unbeaten egg
$\frac{1}{3}$ cup sugar
$\frac{1}{8}$ teaspoon salt
1 cup semi-sweet chocolate morsels
1½ cups flour
1 cup sugar
¼ cup cocoa
1 teaspoon baking soda
½ teaspoon salt
1 cup water
$\frac{1}{3}$ cup cooking oil
1 tablespoon vinegar
1 teaspoon vanilla extract

Preheat oven to 350°F. In a medium bowl, combine the cream
cheese, egg, sugar, and salt. Stir in the chocolate morsels and set
aside. In a separate bowl, sift together the flour, sugar, cocoa, baking soda, and salt. Add the water, oil, vinegar, and vanilla and beat
until well combined. Fill lined muffin cups ⅓ full with the batter.
Top each with a heaping tablespoon of the cream cheese mixture.
Bake 30–35 minutes.

BRAMBLEBERRY B&B

Brambleberry B&B is the perfect place to spend a romantic weekend in the country. The B&B is surrounded by hundreds of acres of farmland and is situated at the end of a peaceful valley. Guests enjoy walking our 80-acres of wooded, creek-side nature trails. Guests can also take our farm tour after breakfast and see the sheep, cattle, chickens, and organic gardens.

As a Travel Green Wisconsin inn, we strive to achieve a large degree of self-sufficiency by growing much of our own food. Guests enjoy our natural, homegrown organic pork products, eggs, fruit, and vegetables. We serve a generous, multi-course, candlelit breakfast in our Scottish-inspired dining room. Breakfast is delivered to your room upon request.

INNKEEPERS: Sherry & Chris Hardie

ADDRESS: N3684 Claire Road, Taylor, WI 54659

TELEPHONE: (608) 525-8001

E-MAIL: innkeeper@brambleberrybandb.com

WEBSITE: www.brambleberrybandb.com

ROOMS: 4 Rooms

CHILDREN: Facility inappropriate for children

PETS: Pet-free environment

Chocolate Liqueur Cake

Makes 1 Cake

"This elegant dessert gets rave reviews from our guests who frequently request this recipe. It's easily adaptable for other liqueurs."
—INNKEEPER, *Brambleberry B&B*

CAKE BATTER
10 tablespoons soft butter
6 tablespoons cocoa
2 eggs
1 cup sugar
1 teaspoon vanilla extract
Dash salt
½ cup flour

LIQUEUR LAYER
1 cup powdered sugar
¼ cup melted butter
2 tablespoons liqueur
 (we recommend raspberry or
 crème de menthe)

CHOCOLATE GLAZE FROSTING
3 tablespoons butter   ¾ cup semi-sweet chocolate chips

For the cake: Preheat oven to 350°F. In a medium bowl, beat together the butter, cocoa, eggs, sugar, vanilla, salt, and flour until well combined. The batter will be thick. Pour into a greased 9 or 10-inch springform pan. Bake 20 minutes, or until a toothpick inserted in the center comes away clean. Allow cake to cool completely before topping with the liqueur layer.

Mix together all of the ingredients for the liqueur layer and spread evenly over the cooled cake. The liqueur layer should firm up before topping with the frosting. To make the frosting, combine the ingredients in a Pyrex cup and melt for one minute in the microwave (high). Stir until all of the chocolate bits are melted and the frosting is glossy. Spread evenly over the firmed liqueur layer and allow to cool.

To serve: Release the springform and cut the cake into 8 slices. Drizzle chocolate syrup over each plate and top with the cake slice. Serve with whipped cream, fresh raspberries or mint leaves, and shaved chocolate.

Garden Gate B&B

"Breakfast is our Signature!" here at the Garden Gate.

Garden Gate is known for its friendly hospitality and elegant breakfasts served every morning in the dining room and accompanied by music and candlelight.

This premier Victorian b&b is located in Door County Wisconsin, often considered the "Cape Cod of the Midwest." This inn sits just two blocks from Sturgeon Bay's historical downtown,  where you'll find the Maritime Museum, the Third Ave Playhouse, shopping on Jefferson Street with its quaint shops, art galleries, and fine restaurants. The county has five state parks, ten lighthouses, and over 300 miles of scenic shoreline to attract artisans, painters, pottery makers, songwriters and a great getaway from everyday life. Stroll along the scenic shorefront and make a sunset memory with someone special. Attend a wooden boat show, a bass or trout tournament, a game of golf, a bicycle ride, a trolley ride, or a fish boil with a piece of cherry pie (Door County favorites!). End your day with an evening dessert and a good night's sleep.

INNKEEPER:	Robin Vallow
ADDRESS:	434 N 3rd Avenue, Sturgeon Bay, WI 54235
TELEPHONE:	(920) 217-3093; (877) 734-9618
E-MAIL:	stay@doorcountybb.com
WEBSITE:	www.doorcountybb.com
ROOMS:	4 Rooms
CHILDREN:	Welcome
PETS:	Pet-free environment

Chocolate Carrot Cake

Makes 12 Servings

"Chocolate lover's delight.
Heads will turn when you bring in this dish;
it's impressive and mouth-watering. Words can't describe this one.
I'm a chocoholic and this is my favorite icing."

—INNKEEPER, *Garden Gate B&B*

2 cups all-purpose flour
2 cups sugar
½ cup baking cocoa
1 teaspoon baking soda
½ teaspoon salt
4 eggs
1¼ cups vegetable oil
3 cups finely shredded carrots

FROSTING
1 (8 ounce) package cream cheese, softened
½ cup butter, softened
3¾ cup confectioners' sugar
¼ cup baking cocoa
3 teaspoons vanilla extract
¼ cup chopped walnuts
¼ cup semi-sweet chocolate chips

Preheat oven to 350°F and line two 9-inch round baking pans with waxed paper. Grease the paper and set aside. In a large mixing bowl, combine the flour, sugar, cocoa, baking soda, and salt. Add the eggs, oil, and carrots and beat until well combined. Pour the batter into the prepared pans and bake 25–30 minutes, or until a toothpick inserted in the center comes out clean. Cool for 10 minutes before removing from pans to wire racks to cool completely.

For the frosting: In a large mixing bowl, beat the cream cheese and butter until fluffy. Beat in the confectioners' sugar, cocoa, and vanilla until smooth. Place one cake layer on a serving plate and spread with half of the frosting. Top with the other cake layer and ice with remaining frosting. Sprinkle with nuts and chocolate chips.

Coloma Hotel

The Coloma Hotel is an historic hotel with modern conveniences. Visitors will experience what it was like to stay at the inn in the early 1900s, when guests could still debark the train at the stop right across the street.

Each room has its own individual décor and history. Play the old player piano or have a drink in the pub to relax. Coloma is a friendly and safe place to relax or participate in sports such as bike riding, hiking, hunting, or fishing. Country life with modern touches! Coloma is also great place for outdoor weddings, reunions, and parties.

INNKEEPERS: Dennis & Susan Apps
ADDRESS: 132 E Main Street, Coloma, WI 54930
TELEPHONE: (715) 228-2401
E-MAIL: info@colomahotel.com
WEBSITE: www.colomahotel.com
ROOMS: 8 Rooms
CHILDREN: Inquire
PETS: Inquire

No Bake Cheesecake

Makes 2 Pies

"This is my husband's favorite cheesecake.
Whenever I make it, he prays the guests won't like it
so he'll have more to eat for himself.
The best thing about it is that there is no baking involved
so it is great in the summer."
—INNKEEPER, *Coloma Hotel*

1 package dream whip
½ cup milk
½ cup powdered sugar
1 (12 ounce) package cream cheese
2 prepared graham cracker crust pie shells
2 cans pie filling (apple, cherry, or blueberry)

Using an electric mixer, prepare the dream whip as directed, using the ½ cup milk. Make sure dream whip peaks. Cream together the sugar and cream cheese until mixed. Mix the dream whip and cream cheese mixture together and divide between the prepared pie shells. Top with the pie filling and refrigerate. Pies are ready for serving.

ALTEMUS CORNERS B&B

Altemus Corners B&B, located in Stoughton, Wisconsin —
only 25 minutes from beautiful Madison — makes a perfect
weekend getaway any time of year. This old-fashioned, 1870's farm
home, situated in the heart of farm country, has been completely
refurbished but still features the original woodwork, layout, and
ambiance. Period antiques and handmade Victorian lampshades
accent every room and fresh flowers can be found throughout the
house.

The southern-style front porch with gazebo is an excellent place
to eat breakfast and relax on warm summer days. A full breakfast
is served each morning and dishes include eggs, meat, pancakes,
Danish kringle, fresh farm fruit and produce, juices, coffee, and tea.
Homemade desserts and beverages are also served in the evening.

INNKEEPER: Marge Stokstad
ADDRESS: 1345 Tower Drive, Stoughton, WI 53589
TELEPHONE: (608) 695-0693
E-MAIL: margestokstad@hotmail.com
WEBSITE: www.altemuscorners.com
ROOMS: 5 Rooms; Private & shared baths
CHILDREN: Children age 12 and older welcome
PETS: Pet-free environment

Cranberry/Strawberry Topped Cheesecake

Makes 1 Pie

"This cheesecake is served regularly at the Altemus Corners B&B. The lemon taste is always fresh in summer or winter with berry topping and it's always wonderful to have a dairy treat for the guests. They sleep really great after an 8 p.m. dessert like this one!"

—INNKEEPER, *Altemus Corners B&B*

1 (8 ounce) bag animal crackers, finely crushed

½ cup butter

1 (8 ounce) package cream cheese, softened

½ cup plus 3 tablespoons sugar, divided

2 eggs

3 tablespoons fresh lemon juice

1½ teaspoons vanilla extract, divided

1½ cups sour cream

Whipped cream

TOPPING

¾ cup fresh cranberries

¾ cup water

2 teaspoons corn starch

¼ cup sugar

¾ cup fresh sliced strawberries

Preheat oven to 325°F. Melt the butter in a glass pie plate. Add the cookie crumbs, mix, and press into the bottom of the plate and up the sides. In a medium bowl, cream together the cream cheese and ½ cup sugar. Add the eggs one at a time. Stir in the lemon and 1 teaspoon vanilla; mix to combine. Pour the cream cheese mixture into the pie plate and bake 20 minutes, or until set. In a medium bowl, mix together the sour cream, 3 tablespoons sugar, and ½ teaspoon vanilla. Remove the cheesecake from the oven and top with the sour cream mixture. Return to oven for an additional 10 minutes. Cool and refrigerate. Serve with whipped cream and berry topping.

For the topping: Boil the cranberries in the water for about 5 minutes. The cranberries will pop. Mix the cornstarch in a bit of cold water to make a thick slurry. Remove the cranberries from heat and add the slurry and sugar. Allow the mixture to cool 10 minutes before adding sliced strawberries.

HILLCREST INN & CARRIAGE HOUSE

Tranquility awaits visitors at The Hillcrest Inn & Carriage House. Guests enter through the gates of the original stone pillars before approaching the 1908 Edwardian estate. A panoramic seven-mile view of waterways is framed by the foliage and flower gardens that abound on this four-acre property. Relaxing on the porches or taking a quiet stroll to the ornate gazebo nestled in the woods are experiences to be treasured.

The main house has been meticulously restored to its original splendor, offering guests warmth, serenity, and beauty. Turn-of-the-century furnishings take guests back in time to a more peaceful and elegant era. Lace curtains on the windows, down comforters on the beds, classical music drifting up the staircase, and the aroma of cinnamon wafting from the oven are sure to please the weary traveler. A formal four-course breakfast, which always includes a taste of chocolate, is served on fine china and stemware in the dining room each morning.

INNKEEPERS: Gayle & Mike Hohner

ADDRESS: 540 Storle Avenue, Burlington, WI 53105

TELEPHONE: (262) 763-4706; (800) 313-9030

E-MAIL: hillcrest@thehillcrestinn.com

WEBSITE: www.thehillcrestinn.com

ROOMS: 6 Rooms

CHILDREN: Inquire

PETS: Pet-free environment

Chocolate Raspberry Brownies

Makes 12 Servings

*"This delightful combination of flavors provides
and impressive dessert after any meal."*
—INNKEEPER, *Hillcrest Inn & Carriage House*

¾ cup butter
3 squares unsweetened chocolate
1½ cups sugar
3 eggs
1 teaspoon vanilla extract
1¼ cups flour
1 (12 ounce) jar seedless raspberry preserves
1 cup semi-sweet chocolate chips
¼ cup half & half

Preheat oven to 350°F and grease a 9x13-inch baking dish. Melt the butter and unsweetened chocolate together in the microwave. Stir in the sugar, eggs, flour, and vanilla and blend well. Spread the mixture in the prepared pan and bake 25 minutes. Remove from oven and cut into 24 pieces. Place 12 of the brownies on a serving platter and spread the raspberry preserves over the top. Cover with a second brownie. In a microwave safe bowl, melt together the semi-sweet chocolate chips and half & half. Drizzle the mixture over the brownies.

Phipps Inn

As owners and innkeepers since September 2000, Mary Ellen and Rich Cox have enjoyed making the bed and breakfast experience at the Phipps Inn one to remember for thousands of guests. Here's what three of them have to say about the inn:

"The house, this room, the décor are all exquisite. It felt like we stepped back in time but with all the modern conveniences!" —GUEST

"It was a great way to unwind and spend our honeymoon. The room, tub, fireplace, and hospitality were more than we expected. The breakfast was possibly the best breakfast we've ever had." —GUEST

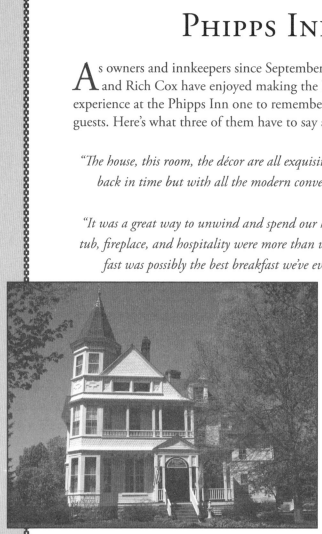

"As usual we had a wonderful and relaxing retreat from everyday life. (There's a reason we keep coming back here — it's simply the best!) Thank you again for your hospitality and amazing breakfast. We'll see you soon!" —GUEST

INNKEEPERS:	Mary Ellen & Rich Cox
ADDRESS:	1005 3rd Street, Hudson, WI 54016
TELEPHONE:	(715) 386-0800
E-MAIL:	info@phippsinn.com
WEBSITE:	www.phippsinn.com
ROOMS:	6 Rooms
CHILDREN:	Inquire
PETS:	Pet-free environment

Phipps Inn Triple Layer Mint Brownies

Makes 50-60 Bars

"Mary Ellen 'invented' these brownies for the Inns of the Valley Chocolate March."

—INNKEEPER, *Phipps Inn*

1 cup sugar
½ cup softened butter
½ teaspoon salt
1 teaspoon vanilla extract
4 eggs
1 cup flour
1 (16 ounce) can Hershey's chocolate syrup

MINT LAYER
3 cups powdered sugar
3 tablespoons milk
5 drops green food coloring
¾ cup softened butter
1 teaspoon peppermint extract

TOPPING
2½ cups semi-sweet chocolate chips
¾ cup butter
3 tablespoons milk

Preheat oven to 350°F and grease an 11x17-inch pan. In a medium bowl, combine the sugar, butter, salt, and vanilla. Mix in the eggs and then add the flour and chocolate syrup. Pour into the prepared pan and bake 20–25 minutes. Cool.

For the mint layer: Mix all of the ingredients together in a large bowl and spread over the cooled brownies. Refrigerate 20 minutes.

For the topping: Melt the chocolate chips and butter together in the microwave. Stir, then add the milk and stir until smooth. Pour over the mint layer and refrigerate until set, about 30 minutes. Cut into bars to serve and store in the refrigerator. These also freeze very well.

OTTER CREEK INN

When you spy this Wisconsin inn from the roadside, you'll be impressed by the charm of its unique setting. Tucked in among huge trees on a wooded hill, the Otter Creek Inn Bed and Breakfast, one of the longest operating Wisconsin b&bs, beckons with a warm welcome. The one-acre wooded lot abounds with flowers in the summer, provides a panorama of colored leaves in the fall, and glistens under a snow-covered blanket during the Wisconsin winter.

This spacious English Tudor three-story inn is decorated in an inviting romantic country Victorian theme. It will enfold you in an aura of yesteryear but will provide you with all the lodging comforts of today. We serve full breakfasts every day of the week.

Our breakfast menu allows a choice of entrees, serving times, and location to dine. You might enjoy your breakfasts in bed, in the privacy of your room, or in the common area.

INNKEEPERS:	Shelley & Randy Hansen
ADDRESS:	2536 HWY 12, Eau Claire, WI 54702
TELEPHONE:	(715) 832-2945; (866) 832-2945
E-MAIL:	info@ottercreekinn.com
WEBSITE:	www.ottercreekinn.com
ROOMS:	6 Rooms
CHILDREN:	Facility inappropriate for children
PETS:	Pet-free environment

Easy Blonde Brownies

Makes 12 Servings

"These are easy to make, just one saucepan and one baking pan,
but are a favorite of young and old."

—INNKEEPER, *Otter Creek Inn*

$^2/_3$ cup margarine

2 cups brown sugar

3 eggs

1 teaspoon vanilla

2 cups flour

1 teaspoon baking powder

1 teaspoon salt

1–1½ cups semi-sweet chocolate chips

Preheat oven to 350°F and grease a 9x13-inch baking dish. Melt
the margarine in a saucepan over low heat. Add the brown sugar
and stir until melted. Beat in the eggs, vanilla, flour, baking powder,
and salt. Spread the batter into the prepared pan and top with
chocolate chips. Bake 25 minutes.

Blondies/butterscotch, are said to have been
invented long before the traditional chocolate
brownie. Brownies were made popular when
the mass production and distribution made
chocolate more affordable, but blondies in
various forms probably date back to the days
of the traditional gingerbread cake.

January 22 is National Blonde Brownie Day!

MILL HOUSE INN

Mill House Inn is a beautiful Victorian home situated on 40 acres of outdoor seclusion and natural beauty on Duck Creek in Rio, Wisconsin. The inn is conveniently located near local attractions, walking trails, canoeing, quaint towns, and historic sites. Whether you are looking for a romantic getaway or simply a way to relax, renew, and restore yourself, Mill House Inn provides the perfect setting for a retreat surrounded by nature.

We offer a gourmet breakfast using local and organic fresh food, Wisconsin cheeses, and chocolates, and offer freshly baked scones, muffins, and hot-out-of-the-oven cookies for an afternoon treat — warm hospitality, relaxing atmosphere, and great food.

INNKEEPER: Lisa Natoli

ADDRESS: W 5384 HWY G, Rio, WI 53960

TELEPHONE: (608) 429-2195

E-MAIL: info@millhousebandb.com

WEBSITE: www.millhousebandb.com

ROOMS: 4 Rooms

CHILDREN: Welcome

PETS: Pet-free environment

Gingersnap Cookies

Makes 4 Dozen

*"I have no idea where this recipe originally came from,
but these cookies usually do not last more than one day.
They are great hot, straight out of the oven."*

—INNKEEPER, Mill House Inn

¾ cup butter or margarine

1 cup sugar

1 egg

¼ cup molasses

2 cups all-purpose flour

2 teaspoons baking soda

¼ teaspoon salt

1 teaspoon cinnamon

1 teaspoon cloves

1 teaspoon ginger

Preheat oven to 375°F. In a medium bowl, cream together the
butter and sugar. Add the egg and molasses and beat well. In a
separate bowl, sift together the flour, baking soda, salt, cinnamon,
cloves, and ginger. Gradually add the dry mixture to the creamed
mixture; mix well. Chill the dough and then roll into 1¼-inch balls.
Dip in additional sugar and place 2 inches apart on ungreased
cookie sheets. Bake 10 minutes, or until set and surface cracks.
Cook on wire racks.

GRAPEVINE LOG CABINS B&B

O ur bed and breakfast consists of three log cabins that each comfortably accommodate up to four people. Grapevine is a quiet romantic getaway for guests looking to relax for a weekend or longer.

Breakfast is served each morning in the main house. Small groups will enjoy sit-down, family-style breakfast and larger parties are served buffet-style. Our guests are always surprised by the great selection and we always get compliments. After breakfast enjoy a walk on our mile-long hiking trail through the woods. We are also located just a mile and a half from the world famous Elroy-Sparta bike trail.

INNKEEPERS:	Ole & Janice Knutson
ADDRESS:	19149 Jade Road, Sparta, WI 54656
TELEPHONE:	(608) 269-3619
E-MAIL:	okgrapevine@centurytel.net
WEBSITE:	www.grapevinelogcabins.com
ROOMS:	3 Cabins
CHILDREN:	Welcome
PETS:	Inquire

Cranberry Cookies

Makes About 80 Cookies

*"This recipe came from my mother. It is very popular at the inn.
I always have them at my open house in my gift shop
and people have come to expect them each year."*
—INNKEEPER, *Grapevine Log Cabins B&B*

1 cup butter	BURNT BUTTER FROSTING
2 cups sugar	1 cup melted butter
1½ cups brown sugar	½ teaspoon vanilla extract
2 eggs	4–6 tablespoons cream
½ cup milk	4 cups powdered sugar
6 cups flour	
2 teaspoons baking powder	
½ teaspoon baking soda	
1 teaspoon salt	
4 cups fresh or frozen cranberries, chopped slightly	
1½–2 cups nuts	

Preheat oven to 375°F. In a large bowl, mix together the butter and sugars. Add the eggs, one at a time, mixing after each addition. Add in the milk and then the flour, baking powder, baking soda, and salt and mix well to combine. Fold in the cranberries and nuts - if you are using frozen cranberries, thaw them slightly in the microwave before adding. Drop the cookies by heaping spoonfuls onto a cookie sheet; do not flatten at all. Bake until cookies begin to tan. Frost with burnt butter frosting.

For the frosting: Brown the butter in a saucepan on the stove. Add the remaining ingredients and stir to combine.

Tips and Variations

This recipe has been doubled, but these cookies freeze very well.

Oscar H. Hanson House B&B

Welcome to the Oscar H. Hanson House Bed & Breakfast, a romantically appointed 1883 Victorian mansion nestled in Cambridge, Wisconsin.

Our spacious porch, comfortable parlor, beautiful gardens, and fountains invite you to stay and bask in the quiet of our inn. Experience the romantic personality of our rooms with in-room breakfast service, fireplaces, stained glass, spacious showers, and claw-foot soaking or Jacuzzi tubs. Feel the passion in your surroundings and recall your commitment to your heart and to that of another. We look forward to your stay and invite you to enjoy the pleasures of our home.

INNKEEPERS: Duke & Mary Jane Mihajlovic

ADDRESS: 303 E North Street, Cambridge, WI 53523

TELEPHONE: (608) 423-4379; (888) 706-7227

E-MAIL: info@ohhanson.com

WEBSITE: www.ohhanson.com

ROOMS: 4 Rooms

CHILDREN: Inquire

PETS: Pet-free environment

Oscar H. Hanson House Signature Cookies

Makes 4 Dozen

1½ cups flour
1 teaspoon baking soda
1 teaspoon cinnamon
½ teaspoon salt
3 cups oatmeal
1 cup butter
1 cup brown sugar
½ cup white sugar
2 eggs
1 teaspoon vanilla extract
1½ cups dried berry mixture

Preheat oven to 350°F. In a medium bowl, mix together the flour, baking soda, cinnamon, salt, and oatmeal. In a separate bowl, cream together the butter and sugars. Add the eggs and vanilla. Mix the dry ingredients into the wet mixture; fold in the dried berries. Scoop rounded tablespoons of dough onto cookie sheets lined with brown parchment paper. Space about 2 inches apart. Sprinkle the tops of the cookies with sugar and flatten the dough balls slightly with the smooth bottom of a spoon greased with butter. Bake 10–12 minutes.

Tips and Variations

For larger cookies, use a larger scoop and adjust baking time accordingly.

Inn at Windmill Farm

Relax in the quiet intimacy of an early 1900 restored farmhouse located in a pastoral setting in the central part of the Door County Peninsula. The Inn at Windmill Farm, featured in *Door County Magazine* and the *Wisconsin Trails* magazine, is situated on ten acres along with the original barn, well house, windmill, and orchard.

The award-winning Inn at Windmill Farm provides you with a step back to a gentler time. The rooms are all air-conditioned and a guest telephone is available in the library, keeping with the quiet atmosphere of the inn, and to make your visit relaxing and peaceful. Windmill Farm is located within easy reach of all Door County has to offer and our goal is to make your stay one of your best experiences ever.

INNKEEPERS: Ed Fenendael & Frank Villigan

ADDRESS: 3829 Fairview Road, Baileys Harbor, WI 54202

TELEPHONE: (920) 868-9282

E-MAIL: windmillfarmwi@aol.com

WEBSITE: www.1900windmillfarm.com

ROOMS: 3 Rooms

CHILDREN: Facility inappropriate for children

PETS: Pet-free environment

Crispy Cookies

Makes about 4 Dozen

1 cup sugar

1 cup brown sugar

1 cup butter

1 cup vegetable oil

1 egg

1 teaspoon vanilla extract

3½ cups flour

1 teaspoon baking soda

1 teaspoon salt

1 teaspoon cream of tartar

1 cup oatmeal

1 cup Rice Crispies

1 cup flaked coconut

½ cup chopped pecans

Preheat oven to 350°F. In a large bowl, cream together the sugar, brown sugar, butter, and vegetable oil. Add in the egg and vanilla and mix to combine. In a separate bowl, sift together the flour, baking soda, salt, and cream of tartar. Add to the creamed mixture and blend well. Stir in the oatmeal, Rice Crispies, coconut, and pecans and drop by teaspoonfuls onto a cookie sheet. Press each cookie with a fork and bake 15 minutes.

Tips and Variations

To make a chocolate version, add in ¾ cup cocoa, 1 extra egg white, ½ cup brown sugar, ½ cup granulated sugar, and $\frac{1}{3}$ cup butter or oil. Follow instructions as above and sprinkle with powdered sugar once the cookies are cool.

PARKVIEW B&B

Parkview B&B, an 1895 Queen Anne Victorian, opened in 1989 in the Park Street Historic District of Reedsburg, Wisconsin. Innkeepers Tom and Donna Hofmann have lovingly restored the home to its original beauty while adding modern conveniences. Stone and shell lawn decorations in the yard, two ponds, a wind-

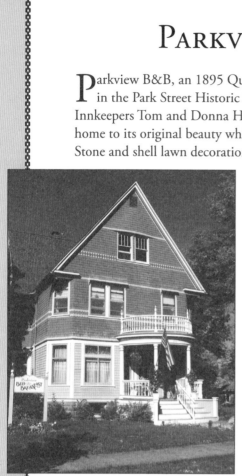

mill, and a lighthouse are the legacy left by the second owner. Inside discover interesting features such as the suitor's window, original woodwork and hardware, hardwood floors, tray ceilings, built-in dining room hutch, and more.

Wake up coffee or tea is available prior to a full, homemade breakfast. Donna, a home economist, prepares seasonal breakfasts using local products and guests often comment on how great the food is.

INNKEEPERS:	Tom & Donna Hofmann
ADDRESS:	211 N Park Street, Reedsburg, WI 53959
TELEPHONE:	(608) 524-4333
E-MAIL:	info@parkviewbb.com
WEBSITE:	www.parkviewbb.com
ROOMS:	4 Rooms; Private & shared baths
CHILDREN:	Inquire
PETS:	Pet-free environment

Orange Craisin Pistachio Biscotti

Makes 24 Cookies

"This is pretty at Christmas time.
I use it on the coffee tray for guests before breakfast."
—INNKEEPER, *Parkview B&B*

½ cup butter, softened
¾ cup sugar
1 tablespoon grated orange zest
½ teaspoon vanilla extract
2 large eggs
2 cups flour
1½ teaspoons baking powder
¼ teaspoon salt
½ cup chopped white chocolate
½ cup Craisins
1¼ cups pistachios, chopped

In a medium bowl, beat together the butter, sugar, orange zest, and vanilla until light and fluffy. Add the eggs one at a time, beating well after each one. In a separate bowl, mix together the flour, baking powder, and salt. Stir the dry ingredients into the butter mixture and chill 30 minutes.

Preheat oven to 325°F. Turn the dough onto a lightly floured surface and divide in half. Shape each half into two flattened logs, about 12 inches long and 3 inches wide. Place the logs on a greased baking sheet at least 3 inches apart. Bake 25–30 minutes, until golden brown. Cool 5 minutes. Cut crosswise, on a diagonal, into 1-inch slices and arrange cut side down on a baking sheet. Bake 8–10 minutes, flip to the other side and bake 5–8 minutes, until golden brown. Transfer to racks to cool.

Wisconsin Bed & Breakfast Association 2008 Innkeeper Cook-off

Wisconsin Bed & Breakfast Association 2008 Innkeeper Cook-off

Our cook-off had all the drama
and suspense you'd expect
from one of those reality-cooking shows,
with cranberries as the secret ingredient.

SPECKLED HEN INN
Wisconsin Breakfast Panini

Makes 4 Servings

"This grilled breakfast sandwich is filled with the bounty of our state; baby Swiss cheese, applewood smoked bacon, crisp red apple slices, and our homemade cranberry-cherry chutney. This recipe is easily scalable for any number of servings. You will need to use a panini press or heavy skillet to make this."

—INNKEEPER, *The Speckled Hen Inn*

8 slices country Italian bread

8 thin slices baby Swiss cheese

8 slices applewood smoked bacon,
    cooked until crisp

1 large red crisp apple, cored
    and thinly sliced

4 tablespoons cranberry-cherry chutney,
    (recipe follows)

Melted butter for grilling

Assemble the sandwiches by stacking the ingredients in the following order: 1 slice bread, 1 slice cheese, 2 slices bacon, apple slices, and another slice of cheese. Spread 1 tablespoon of chutney on the final slice of bread and place it, chutney-side-down on the sandwich. Repeat the process for the other three sandwiches. Brush the outer side of the bread slices with melted butter. Place in the panini press and grill until the bread is golden brown and the cheese has melted. This may also be done in a heavy skillet by carefully flipping the sandwich to cook on both sides. Cut the sandwiches in half or quarters and serve warm with additional chutney if desired.

Cranberry-Cherry Chutney

1 cup water
1 cup sugar
12 ounces cranberries, fresh or frozen
½ cup cider vinegar
1 cup dried Door County cherries
1 teaspoon Penzey's Baking Spice
   (a blend of cinnamon, cassia, anise,
   allspice, mace, and cardamom)
1 peeled cored apple, diced

Bring the water and sugar to a boil in a medium saucepan. Add the remaining ingredients and return to a boil. Reduce the heat and simmer 15 minutes, until the apple is tender and the cranberries have popped. Cool and refrigerate.

To serve: At breakfast, the panini is often served as a side dish with scrambled eggs with cream cheese and herbs. Garnish with fresh herbs and additional apple slices. It is also great in a breakfast-to-go bag for early morning departures.

OLD RITTENHOUSE INN
Wisconsin Cranberry "Borscht" with Bison Strip Steak

Makes 4 Servings

"This entrée was inspired by the individuality of the three main flavors — cranberries, bison, and beets — the warmth they create when combined, and the color red."
—INNKEEPER, *Old Rittenhouse Inn*

BORSCHT
2¼ cups rich beef stock
3 tablespoons red wine vinegar
1½ cups peeled red beets,
    cut into small wedges or large dice
1 carrot, peeled and cut in large dice
1½ cups fresh cranberries
2 tablespoons sugar
1 cup finely shredded cabbage
Kosher salt and freshly ground pepper,
    to taste
4 tablespoons butter

In a medium saucepan, bring the stock, beets, vinegar, and a pinch of salt to a boil. Simmer over medium heat until beets are tender, about 25 minutes. This recipe can be done a day in advance up to this point and brought back to a simmer at service time. This is also the perfect time to start preparing the bison. Add the carrots and simmer 5 minutes more. Add the cranberries, sugar, and cabbage and simmer 3 minutes. While simmering, swirl in the butter, taste and adjust with more sugar, salt, and pepper.

BISON
1½ pounds bison NY strip loin,
    neatly trimmed
4 sprigs fresh thyme
2 tablespoons cold butter
Kosher salt, to taste
Fresh ground white pepper,
    to taste
1 tablespoon vegetable oil

Preheat oven to 350°F. Season the bison with salt and pepper and heat a heavy, oven-proof frying pan until quite hot. Add the thyme and the butter to the pan, scraping the brown bits into the butter. Place the steak on top of the thyme sprigs and place the entire pan in the oven until the meat reaches desired doneness. Recommend rare to medium rare for best flavor and texture, about 10 minutes. Bison is very lean and will cook more quickly than beef. Let rest in a warm place 5 minutes before serving.

To serve: Remove the bison steak to a serving board and slice across the grain. Place a portion of mashed potatoes onto warmed plates. Carefully spoon the borscht onto the center of each plate and arrange the bison over the top, against the potatoes. Top with a dollop of crème fraîche and a sprinkle of fresh dill.

WESTBY HOUSE VICTORIAN INN
Waffles with Cranberry Topping & Cinnamon Cream Syrup

Makes 8 Servings

"This combination of cranberries and waffles adds warmth to a fall breakfast. The thin cinnamon cream syrup puts a nice light finish to the meal."

—INNKEEPER, *Westby House Victorian Inn*

1 cup fresh or frozen cranberries
2 cups tart apples, pared and diced
1½ cups sugar
⅛ teaspoon cinnamon
¼ teaspoon nutmeg
⅛ teaspoon ground cloves
½ cup water, divided
2 tablespoons cornstarch
½ cup coarsely broken walnuts for garnish
1 cup whipping cream, (optional)

CINNAMON CREAM SYRUP
2 cups brown sugar
½ cup light corn syrup
¼ cup water
¾ cup evaporated milk
1 teaspoon vanilla extract
½ teaspoon cinnamon

Make your favorite waffle recipe and bake on a waffle iron. Keep warm until served. Combine the first six ingredients, and ¼ cup water in a medium saucepan. Heat, stirring occasionally, to boiling then cook 5 minutes. Mix the cornstarch into the remaining ¼ cup water to make a smooth slurry; stir into the cranberry mixture. Cook, stirring constantly, until the mixture thickens and boils. Divide evenly over the waffles.

For the syrup: In a medium saucepan, combine the brown sugar, corn syrup, and water. Bring the mixture to a boil and stir for 2 minutes to thicken. Remove from heat and stir in the remaining ingredients. To serve ladle a small amount onto a serving plate and top with a waffle. Add the cranberry topping to the center of each waffle and ladle with additional syrup. Garnish with walnuts and fresh whipping cream. A side order of lime-pepper seasoned bacon is a great complement.

HONORABLE MENTION

AUGUSTA
VICTORIAN ROSE B&B
Sunshine Waffles with
Easy Cranberry Sauce

Makes 4 Servings

"This is a family favorite."
—INNKEEPER, *Augusta Victorian Rose B&B*

1 cup orange juice
4 eggs, separated
1 cup flour
Dash of salt
1 tablespoon sugar
1½ teaspoons baking powder

CRANBERRY SAUCE
1 jar Gingerbread Jersey
   Cranberry Apple Jam
Zest from 1 orange
Supremes from 1 orange*
¼ cup sugar, to taste
1 teaspoon fresh grated ginger,
   to taste
1½ cups fresh or frozen cranberries

For the waffles: Preheat a waffle iron. In a medium bowl, beat together the orange juice and egg yolks. In a separate bowl, stir together the dry ingredients. In another separate bowl, beat the egg whites until stiff. Combine the juice/yolk mix with the dry mix until well blended. Gently fold in the egg whites. Pour the mixture into the waffle iron and cook until golden brown. Serve hot with cranberry sauce and sweet cream.

For the sauce: Mix together all of the sauce ingredients in a saucepan over medium-low heat. Heat until the cranberries are cooked through.

Tips and Variations

*To supreme the orange, remove the rind and the white pith. Hold the orange in your hand and run the blade of the knife down each section. Theses are the supremes.

COBBLESTONE B&B
Cranberry Frappè Smoothie

Makes 2 Servings

"My Frappè was generated by my guests!
I always serve a banana orange frappè.
It was cranberry fest and my guests came back
talking about cranberries, so I thought it would be memorable
for them to have Banana Orange Cranberry Frappè."
—INNKEEPER, *Cobblestone B&B*

3 cups fresh squeezed orange juice
1 banana
½ cup fresh cranberries
½ cup shaved ice

Place the ingredients together in a blender and mix to desired consistency.

JUSTIN TRAILS
B&B RESORT
Raw Cran-Apple Orange Relish

Makes 8 Servings

"This recipe was made at a kindergarten where I was student teaching many years ago. This is an annual favorite of our family and guests. I prefer using raw fruit to preserve all of the nutrients and vitamins. We serve this from October until April, with cranberries purchased from my friend, Nodji Van Wychen of Weatherby Cranberries, and apples from local orchards."

—INNKEEPER, *Justin Trails B&B Resort*

2 red apples
2 naval oranges, peeled or unpeeled
2 cups cranberries, fresh or frozen
½ cup honey
1 tablespoon lemon juice
1 cup Craisins

GARNISH
1 (8 ounce) can light
  whipped cream topping
¾ cup chocolate sundae syrup
1 cup Craisins

Wash the fruit, quarter and remove the seeds. Cut each fruit quarter into 8 pieces and place in a food processor. Add the cranberries and process to desired texture. Pour into a mixing bowl. Add the honey, lemon juice, and Craisins and mix. Refrigerate until ready to serve. Scoop into a stemmed goblet or serve family-style on a large serving dish. Top with whipped cream, chocolate sauce, and additional Craisins.

Tips and Variations

This tastes even better after a day in the refrigerator. It is also delicious on salad greens for lunch, as a side dish for dinner, or as we serve it, for breakfast with granola and yogurt.

WESTPORT B&B
Cranberry Nut Muffins

Makes 12 Large or 20 Regular Muffins

*"This recipe has been a family favorite for many years.
We serve these muffins at our b&b and keep bags
of seasonal berries in the freezer so that we can make
these delicious and attractive muffins any time of the year."*

—*INNKEEPER, Westport B&B*

1½ cups coarsely chopped cranberries
1¼ cups sugar, divided
3 cups sifted all-purpose flour
4½ teaspoons baking powder
½ teaspoon salt
½ cup butter
2–3 teaspoons grated orange or lemon peel
2 large eggs
1 cup milk
1 cup chopped pecans or walnuts

Preheat oven to 400°F and spray or line muffin cups. In a small bowl, combine the chopped cranberries and ¼ cup sugar. In a large bowl, mix the remaining sugar, flour, baking powder, and salt until well combined. Using a pastry blender, cut in the butter until the mixture is crumbly; add the grated lemon peel. In a small bowl, beat together the eggs and milk. Add to the flour mixture, stirring just until the dry ingredients are moistened. Fold in the cranberries and nuts and spoon the batter into the muffin cups, filling just ¾ of the way. Bake 20–30 minutes, depending on muffin size, or until a toothpick inserted in the center comes away clean and the tops are lightly browned. Sprinkle or lightly dip warm muffins in a small dish of sugar about 5 minutes after cooking.

LINDSAY HOUSE B&B
Cranberry Walnut Scones

Makes 15 Scones

"I have made a variation of this recipe in the past
to rave reviews from my guests!"
—INNKEEPER, *Lindsay House B&B*

4 cups plus 1 tablespoon flour
2–4 tablespoons sugar,
   plus additional for sprinkling
2 tablespoons baking powder
3 sticks cold butter, diced
4 eggs
1 cup cold heavy cream
¾ cup dried cranberries
¼–½ cup chopped toasted walnuts
2 tablespoons orange zest
1 egg beaten
   with a splash of heavy cream

Preheat oven to 400°F. In a bowl, mix together the flour, sugar, and baking powder. Cut in the butter until pea-sized pieces form. In a separate bowl, combine the eggs and heavy cream. Quickly add the mixture to the batter and mix until just blended. Toss the cranberries in some flour and add to the dough along with the walnuts and orange zest. Pat dough out until approximately ½–1 inch thick. Cut the scones using a biscuit or square cutter and place them on a parchment-lined cookie sheet. Brush the tops with the egg/cream mixture and sprinkle with sugar. Bake 20–25 minutes. Serve with whipped butter and jam.

A Victorian Swan On Water
Kinda Healthy Breakfast Cookies

Makes 4-5 Dozen

"I have been making chocolate chip cookies for years for the bikers on our Christmas Chipmunk Trail Package. This is an original recipe to highlight our area and our state as the largest producer of cranberries."

—Innkeeper, *A Victorian Swan on Water*

¼ cup butter
¾ cup butter flavored shortening
2 jumbo fresh farm eggs
1 cup brown sugar
⅓ cup white sugar
1 teaspoon orange zest
1 teaspoon vanilla extract
1 tablespoon orange juice concentrate
1 cup white flour
½ cup whole wheat flour
¼ teaspoon baking soda
½ teaspoon salt
1 teaspoon cinnamon
¼ teaspoon freshly ground nutmeg
1½ cups old-fashioned oatmeal
½ cup orange flavored Craisins
1 cup lightly toasted almonds, chopped or sliced
1 (5 ounce) high-quality dark chocolate bar, chopped

Preheat oven to 350°F. In a large bowl, cream together the butter and shortening. Beat in the eggs. Add the sugars, orange zest, vanilla, and orange concentrate and mix thoroughly. In a separate bowl, combine the flours, baking soda, salt, cinnamon, and nutmeg. Add the dry ingredients to the creamed mixture and mix to combine. Fold in the oatmeal, Craisins, almonds, and chocolate. Drop by heaping tablespoons (or using an ice cream scoop) on cookie sheets and bake 10–14 minutes, until golden. Remove from pan and cool.

BOWMAN'S OAK HILL B&B
Cranberry Orange Dream French Toast

Plan ahead, this dish needs to be refrigerated overnight!

Makes 4 Servings

7 large eggs
3 cups half & half
8 1½-inch slices dense
   French bread
2 tablespoons butter

CRANBERRY SAUCE
1½ cups fresh or
   frozen cranberries*
¾ cup sugar

ORANGE SAUCE
1 (15 ounce) can Mandarin oranges, drained
1 cup heavy cream
¾ cup sugar

For the French toast: Butter or spray a 9x13-inch baking dish. Combine the eggs and half & half and pour a small amount in the dish. Put the bread in a single layer in the pan. Pour the remaining egg mixture over the bread and let stand 5 minutes. Turn the slices over, cover, and refrigerate overnight.

The following morning: Blend the orange sauce ingredients together in a blender until smooth and slightly thickened. Pour into another container and set aside. Wash blender out and blend cranberry sauce ingredients using a small amount of cranberry juice to thin if necessary. Set aside. Preheat oven to 350°F. Melt butter in a skillet over medium heat and cook the French Toast until golden brown on both sides. Transfer to a non-stick baking sheet and bake 5–7 minutes until puffy.

To assemble, pour ¼ cup orange juice in the middle of the plate. Place 1 or 2 slices of French Toast on top of the sauce and dust with powered sugar. Garnish with dried cranberries and chopped pecans. Drizzle cranberry sauce over top and place a mint leaf in the center.

*If using frozen cranberries, you may need to add a little cranberry juice.

Parkview B&B
Stuffed Cranberry French Toast

Makes 6-8 Servings

"After being served a similar entrée at a b&b a number of years ago, I came home and thought, 'I think I can figure out how to make this dish!' I recreated the recipe with a few twists of my own. I prepare seasonal breakfasts using local foods as much as possible for my guests."

—INNKEEPER, *Parkview B&B*

1 (16 ounce) loaf French bread
4 eggs
1¼ cups milk

FILLING
8 ounces cream cheese
¼ cup finely chopped cranberries, fresh or frozen
¼ cup powdered sugar
¼ cup finely chopped pecans

CRANBERRY SAUCE
1½ cups water or red wine
1 cup sugar
1 stick cinnamon, (optional)
12 ounces fresh or frozen cranberries
2 pears, peeled and sliced

Trim the ends off the bread and slice 1-inch thick. Make a second slice about ¾ through each slice to create a pocket. Beat the eggs and milk together and set aside. In a medium bowl, combine the filling ingredients. Using a table knife, spread 1–2 tablespoons of the cream cheese filling in each bread pocket. Then dip each filled bread slice in the egg mixture and allow it to soak into the bread. You can freeze the French toast at this point if desired. Heat a griddle to 300°F and cook 10–12 minutes. Turn the slices over and cook an additional 10–12 minutes. Both sides should be nicely browned and the cream cheese filling should be heated through. Place two pieces of French toast on a plate and spoon the cranberry sauce over the top. Serve with pork sausage.

For the sauce: Combine the first three ingredients in a 1½-quart saucepan. Bring the mixture to a boil and then add the cranberries and pears. Cook until the cranberries pop and the pears are tender, about 10 minutes. Remove the cinnamon stick. This can be made ahead of time, refrigerated, and then reheated before putting it on the French toast.

CANYON ROAD INN
Wild Rice Craisin Quiche

Makes 6 Servings

"Visitors to Northern Wisconsin enjoy specialty foods
to this area — wild rice, cheese, and cranberries,
which are incorporated in this favorite dish."

—INNKEEPER, *Canyon Road Inn*

1 9-inch pie crust
1 cup wild rice
½ cup Craisins
1 cup shredded Monterey Jack cheese
3 large eggs
1½ cups half & half or milk
1 tablespoon butter

Preheat oven to 425°F. Lay the unbaked pie crust in a quiche pan, do not prick. Bake 5 minutes. Remove the crust from the oven and dot with butter. Reduce oven temperature to 350°F. Prepare the wild rice according to package directions. Layer the wild rice, Craisins, and cheese in the crust. In a medium bowl, beat together the eggs and half & half. Pour the egg mixture over the layers in the crust. Bake 50 minutes, or until the center of the quiche is firm. Cut into wedges and serve.

Tips and Variations

Cook the whole package of wild rice and freeze in easy-to-use 1-cup portions. Thaw in the refrigerator the night before.

Regional Index of Inns

East Wisconsin Waters/Door County

Southwest Hidden Valleys

CONTINUED NEXT PAGE

Alphabetical List of Inns

Recipe Index

Travel Green logo courtesy of Travel Green Wisconsin. Certified Travel Green inns are committed to environmental, social, and economic sustainability. Each inn bearing this logo has been reviewed and certified by the Travel Green Wisconsin program.

9   8   7   6   5   4   3   2

ISBN 978-1-889593-24-1

PUBLISHED BY:
3D Press
a Big Earth Publishing company
1637 Pearl Street, Suite 201
Boulder, CO 80302

800-258-5830 (order toll free)
303-443-9687 (fax)
www.bigearthpublishing.com

FRONT COVER PHOTO: top: Speckled Hen Inn; bottom: Honeybee Inn B&B
BACK COVER PHOTOS: top and middle: Courtesy WBBA; bottom: von Stiehl Winery
COVER AND TEXT DESIGN: Rebecca Finkel
EDITING: Becky LeJeune
PRINTED IN China By Global PSD

 The Bed & Breakfast Cookbook Series was originated by Carol Faino & Doreen Hazledine of Peppermint Press in Denver, Colorado in 1996.